T0318909

Cambridge Elements ☰

Elements in Quantitative Finance
edited by
Riccardo Rebonato
EDHEC Business School

THE BEHAVIORAL ECONOMICS AND POLITICS OF GLOBAL WARMING

Unsettling Behaviors

Hersh Shefrin
Santa Clara University

CAMBRIDGE
UNIVERSITY PRESS

Shaftesbury Road, Cambridge CB2 8EA, United Kingdom

One Liberty Plaza, 20th Floor, New York, NY 10006, USA

477 Williamstown Road, Port Melbourne, VIC 3207, Australia

314–321, 3rd Floor, Plot 3, Splendor Forum, Jasola District Centre,
New Delhi – 110025, India

103 Penang Road, #05–06/07, Visioncrest Commercial, Singapore 238467

Cambridge University Press is part of Cambridge University Press & Assessment,
a department of the University of Cambridge.

We share the University's mission to contribute to society through the pursuit of
education, learning and research at the highest international levels of excellence.

www.cambridge.org
Information on this title: www.cambridge.org/9781009454902

DOI: 10.1017/9781009454919

First published 2023

A catalogue record for this publication is available from the British Library

ISBN 978-1-009-45490-2 Hardback
ISBN 978-1-009-45489-6 Paperback
ISSN 2631-8571 (online)
ISSN 2631-8563 (print)

Additional resources for this publication at www.cambridge.org/shefrin_resources

The Behavioral Economics and Politics of Global Warming

Unsettling Behaviors

Elements in Quantitative Finance

DOI: 10.1017/9781009454919
First published online: October 2023

Hersh Shefrin
Santa Clara University

Author for correspondence: Hersh Shefrin, hshefrin@scu.edu

Abstract: The main goal of this Element is to provide a psychological explanation for why actual global climate policy is so greatly at odds with the prescriptions of most neoclassical economists. To be sure, the behavioral approach does focus on why neoclassical models are often psychologically unrealistic. However, in this Element the author argues that the unrealistic elements are minor compared to the psychological pitfalls driving politically determined climate policy. Why this is the case is what the author describes as the "big behavioral question." More precisely, the big behavioral question asks about unsettling behaviors, why there is a huge gap between actual policy and even the weakest of the prescriptions in the range of plausible recommendations coming from neoclassical economists' integrated assessment models. This title is also available as Open Access on Cambridge Core.

Keywords: warming, irrational, behavioral, fear, hope

ISBNs: 9781009454902 (HB), 9781009454896 (PB), 9781009454919 (OC)
ISSNs: 2631-8571 (online), 2631-8563 (print)

Contents

An online appendix for this publication can be accessed at www.cambridge.org/shefrin_resources

1 Introduction

The interplay between psychology and politics, not economic cost-benefit analysis, has been the key driver of real-world climate policy, and the consequences are unsettling. Actual policies have been more in line with business-as-usual behaviors than with the recommendations made by most mainstream climate scientists and economists. Why psychology and politics have combined to produce this state of affairs is what I call the "big behavioral question."

The psychology of climate change centers on fear, bias, and hope. In a nutshell, fear relates to the kind of future damages that global warming will bring. Bias is about misjudgments and misplaced emotions that hamper the global community from appropriately responding to climate threats. Hope is about the potential emergence of new technologies that might significantly reduce greenhouse gas (GHG) concentrations to sustainable levels in a timely manner at reasonable cost.

1.1 Drivers of the Global Community's Response to Global Warming

Fear, bias, and hope have driven, and will continue to drive, the global community's response to global warming.[1] There is plenty to fear. Thus far, the global community's reaction to most mainstream climate scientists' global warning prognostications and alerts has been too little, too late. The global community has also ignored policy recommendations from mainstream environmental economists about putting incentives in place to induce abatement behavior. While there are many ways to address global warming, business-as-usual behavior is not one of them. Yet, for the most part, over the past four decades global GHG emissions have pretty much followed a business-as-usual trajectory. This is unsettling.

Pitfalls stemming from psychological biases have played a major role in explaining why the global community has resisted the advice from mainstream climate scientists and economists. This is unsettling. Examples of pertinent biases are present bias, confirmation bias, excessive optimism, and overconfidence. Among these, I would single out self-control issues related to present bias, whereby the needs of the present are accorded excessive importance relative to the needs of the future. While we cannot turn back the clock, the community needs to understand biases and their impact on climate policy in

---

[1] I made this point in Hersh Shefrin, *Ending the Illusion of Management* (New York: McGraw-Hill, 2008). The focus of the book was on the psychological dimension of organizational decision-making, and the factors that distinguish organizations that act in psychologically smart ways from others.

order to behave more sensibly going forward. Until the community accepts this reality and successfully addresses it, these biases will continue to contribute to climate havoc.

There is hope for sensibly addressing global warming and restoring GHG concentrations to sustainable levels. Hope rests in the development of nascent technologies for removing GHGs from the atmosphere at reasonable cost. Given the psychological biases preventing the institution of cost-benefit–based emission abatement policies and more investment in adaptation to rising temperatures, the global community will need to rely on GHG removal technologies.

My message of hope for the future needs to be tempered with caution: call the combination cautious hope. The community needs to understand how biases have the potential to reduce the benefit of GHG removal technologies, and the community needs to be prepared to mitigate the potential negative effects from psychological biases.

To identify the impact of fear, bias, and hope on global warming, I focus on three elements. These are:

1. the warnings from most mainstream **climate scientists** about anthropogenic global warming during the past four decades;
2. the prescriptions from economic **integrated assessment models** about cost-benefit–based responses to the threat posed by anthropogenic global warming; and
3. actual climate policy developed in the **political arena**, including the impact of special business interests.

Next I offer comments about each element in turn.

1.2 Climate Scientists

Beginning in 1979 climate scientists provided a coherent analysis of the risks associated with anthropogenic global warming. I use the term "risks" here because these scientists were clear about which statements they were confident in making and which not. In respect to their most important assertion – about the relationship between global temperature and emissions of carbon dioxide – they provided confidence intervals.

People who routinely set unduly narrow confidence intervals are said to be overconfident about their knowledge. More than forty years later climate scientists' key confidence interval has withstood the test of time, suggesting that they were *not* overconfident in their associated judgments.

This is important, as for years climate skeptics maintained that the science underlying global warming is "unsettled." The "unsettled" contention is itself unsettling. Scientific claims are rarely 100 percent settled, so the "unsettled" issue is not germane. Rather, the point is that the science underlying global warming is sufficiently settled to move forward with cost-benefit–based climate policy, with which past policies have been inconsistent. Just to be clear: more than two-thirds of anthropogenic cumulative emissions of carbon dioxide into the atmosphere have occurred since 1979.

1.3 Integrated Assessment Models

Integrated assessment models (IAMs) provide a framework for analyzing alternative economic policy responses to deal with anthropogenic global warming. Economist William Nordhaus developed the first IAM during the 1980s and 1990s, and named his framework the Dynamic Integrated Climate-Economy (DICE) model.[2]

I use DICE as a vehicle for identifying key behavioral issues associated with climate policies. In this respect, Nordhaus identifies two specific policies, one representing business-as-usual behavior and the other representing an optimal response to global warming. I treat the first policy as reflecting the theoretical impact of psychological pitfalls relative to Nordhaus' optimal policy.

There has been wide disagreement among economists about Nordhaus' choice of parameter values and functional forms for computing the optimal solution. Some economists, most prominently Sir Nicholas Stern, propose a much stronger climate policy than Nordhaus' optimal policy.

I will discuss the associated debate in some detail, but at this stage I want readers to understand the following point. Over the course of the past four decades, carbon dioxide emissions have been much closer to the trajectory in Nordhaus' behavioral business-as-usual case than his optimal case. The gap is that much wider for the optimal paths associated with alternative IAMs offered by other economists. This is unsettling.

All of this is to say that when it comes to the formulation of economic policy, policymakers have paid little heed to the recommendations made by eminent economists. This, I suggest, is the result of psychological bias.

The term "neoclassical" can be loaded. The economics profession uses it to characterize the mainstream approach of modeling economic choices as the

---

[2] The DICE model is developed in William Nordhaus, *Managing the Global Commons: The Economics of Climate Change* (Cambridge, MA: MIT Press, 1994). Further elaboration can be found in William Nordhaus, with Paul Sztorc, *DICE User's Manual*, second edition, 2013. https://tinyurl.com/5n6zwua3. Also see the dicemodel.net website. Information about the 2016 version of the DICE model can be found in William Nordhaus, "Revisiting the Social Cost of Carbon," *Proceedings of the National Science Foundation* 114(7) (2017), 1518–1523. www.pnas.org/doi/10.1073/pnas.1609244114.

outcome of rational decision-making; this is how I use the term throughout this Element. I understand that some readers might use the term more broadly – for example, as a label for a libertarian-based approach – but my definition is narrower.

Nordhaus constructed DICE as a neoclassical framework by introducing climate equations into the production sector of a traditional aggregate growth model. His model features a representative agent/social planner, meaning that the economy behaves *as if* all agents/consumers have the same preferences. The optimal case corresponds to the representative agent engaging in maximizing behavior, which is to say that the representative agent behaves rationally.

There is a tradition in the neoclassical approach of explaining real-world choices through the use of a rational representative agent. Consider two points about this tradition. The first is that the underlying aggregation approach rests on very shaky theoretical ground. The second is that neoclassical assumptions do not capture key psychological aspects of the way real-world individuals behave, especially in respect to intertemporal choice.

The aggregation assumption is that equilibrium can be described as if all agents share the same beliefs and preferences as some average agent, called the representative agent. This is the case even when there is considerable diversity among individual agents in respect to time preference (meaning degree of impatience), risk tolerance, and probabilistic beliefs about different risks. Most importantly, the neoclassical assumption holds that the representative agent is rational. In particular, the representative agent exhibits maximizing behavior, does not change their mind over time, has a stable attitude toward risk, and holds coherent, unbiased beliefs about the risks being faced. By coherent, I mean the holding of consistent conditional probabilities over time.

The neoclassical rationality assumption is heroic. In the general case involving agent diversity in respect to time preference, risk tolerance, and beliefs, the representative agent associated with an equilibrium will not be rational. Instead, the representative agent typically exhibits strong behavioral features. Specifically, the representative agent will be dynamically inconsistent in the sense of wanting to change their mind over time, have an unstable attitude toward bearing risk, and hold biased incoherent beliefs about the risks being faced.[3]

There is a point here about what I call "excessive rationality-assumption bias" in economic modeling. When psychological pitfalls are strong, neoclassical models that exhibit excessive rationality-assumption bias are prone to be misleading.

[3] See Hersh Shefrin, *A Behavioral Approach to Asset Pricing*, second edition (Boston, MA: Elsevier, 2008).

Keep in mind that the concept of a representative agent is an analytical device for analyzing prices and aggregate quantities. In Nordhaus' DICE model the representative agent plays two roles. The first relates to driving private-sector decisions about consumption, saving, and investment. The second relates to public policy about pricing carbon dioxide emissions, which is typically achieved using either a carbon tax or a cap-and-trade system.

Nordhaus constructed DICE to feature two sets of controls, one relating to saving rates and the other to the price of carbon (dioxide). Both of these control variables involve self-control issues featuring present bias, the "unwarranted" overweighting of the present relative to the future. There is certainly a large economics literature on the topic of insufficient saving, and in this Element I will analyze present bias issues associated with pricing carbon.

Nordhaus constructed DICE so that the optimal case produces saving behavior and rates of return on capital that are in line with their respective historical rates. In practice, these historical rates have been relatively stable over time. Whether or not past saving rates qualify as being optimal, there is reason to have confidence that the output from DICE would feature reasonable predictions of saving rates in the future.

The situation with outputs from DICE for carbon prices is another matter. Real-world carbon prices have been significantly less than the "optimal" values generated from DICE. I attribute the gap between the two to present bias associated with a lack of self-control and related psychological pitfalls. Critics of DICE have raised questions about parameter values or functional forms associated with the relationship between damages and atmospheric carbon dioxide concentrations. These are certainly important. However, they miss the important point that DICE fails to capture the psychological pitfalls associated with the political processes that determine the choice of carbon prices and related abatement activity levels.

From a psychological perspective, neoclassical economic models are crude. While consumption/saving decisions and carbon pricing decisions both involve intertemporal self-control issues, neoclassical models fail to capture important nuances differentiating the two. Behavioral economists emphasize that many factors influence self-control, which cannot always be boiled down to a discount rate reflecting time preference and an associated maximization. The difference between saving behavior and emissions abatement behavior is a case in point. This difference is an important issue that I address in this Element.

Similar statements apply to risk. Rather than positing that risk preferences can be captured by a parameter associated with risk aversion, as is the case with the neoclassical approach, the psychology of risk focuses on the way attitude to risk varies across circumstances.[4] This difference is also a topic I address in this Element.

Being a model, DICE is like a heuristic, and a valuable heuristic at that. In terms of structure, it does not capture all the important elements associated with climate policy, but it does provide a robust vehicle for engaging in a systematic discussion about key policy issues. Certainly some of its assumptions about parameter values and functional forms are questionable, but discussing debates about these assumptions provides an opportunity to highlight other critical issues. Being a neoclassical model, its treatment of key psychological elements is crude, but it provides a good starting point for a discussion about which psychological elements are missing and how these missing elements might impact key conclusions from the model.

Although I devote a lot of space to discussing DICE, I want to emphasize that this Element is not primarily about IAMs. It is about the psychology of global warming. Of course, I will discuss weaknesses in DICE and how more recent IAMs have addressed these weaknesses. However, my main reason for doing so is to bring out important psychological issues. These are issues that for the most part neoclassical IAMs miss.

Collectively, IAMs provide a broad range of cost-benefit–based global policies for addressing the threats posed by anthropogenic global warming. Operationally, "cost-benefit based" means a solution to a specific social planning optimization problem. For several reasons, the range is broad, not the least being the amount of uncertainty being faced.

With this said, remember that real-world emissions behavior has been much closer to business as usual than to any of the optimal trajectories from IAMs. Thus far, IAMs might be normative, but they have not been remotely descriptive.

Economists might be speaking, but global decision makers have not been listening, at least when it comes to climate policy. Moreover, developing IAMs with increased complexity is unlikely to lead global decision makers to listen

---

[4] My papers with Richard Thaler on self-control contain the first formal exposition of the two-system thinking fast and slow perspective Kahneman popularized in his outstanding 2011 book. See Daniel Kahneman, *Thinking, Fast and Slow* (New York: Farrar, Straus, and Giroux, 2011). Thaler and I first presented our framework to Kahneman and Tversky in February 1978, when two-system thinking was not part of their approach. Thaler and I called our framework "the planner-doer model," which I maintain provides a better description of the action-based tasks associated with the two systems. It begins with thinking, but it is more than thinking, as thinking gets translated into action. Thaler and I designed the planner-doer framework to analyze self-control issues in economic decision-making. When in 2017 the Nobel Committee presented the award to Thaler in Stockholm, they emphasized our work on the planner-doer model and the way it integrated the major themes in Adam Smith's two major works, connecting them through modern behavioral economics.

more intently to what economists prescribe. More facts and theories are unlikely to make a difference, because the underlying impediments are not for the most part rational: they are psychological.

1.4 Politics

Real-world emissions behavior is the result of decisions made in the spheres of politics and business. Political outcomes are not easily described as optimal policies resulting from choices made by a rational benevolent social planner. In many ways, diversity, meaning heterogeneous beliefs and preferences, operates on political decisions as it does on economic and financial decisions. Political decisions might resemble the outcome of a representative social planner, but this planner exhibits strong behavioral features such as dynamic inconsistency of preferences, biased judgments, and incoherent probability beliefs.

I will make the case that heterogeneity has been a major factor in American climate policy, beginning with the response to the concerns expressed by mainstream climate scientists during 1979. At that time the United States was the largest annual emitter of carbon dioxide into the atmosphere, followed by the Soviet Union. By 1991 the Soviet Union had disintegrated and was subsequently replaced as the second largest emitter by the countries making up the European Union (EU).

On a cumulative basis, the United States has been the leading contributor of carbon dioxide emissions, having emitted about 417 billion metric tons (as of 2021). The EU is second, having contributed about 367 billion tons. Next comes China, which contributed about 238 billion tons.[5]

Notably, as China successfully grew its economy during the past three decades, its carbon dioxide emissions soared. In contrast, the United States and the EU managed to slow their emissions to the point where both had peaked by 2007. Thereafter, on an annual basis, China became the world's largest emitter of carbon dioxide. This has been a major reason why the global community has continued to follow business-as-usual behavior.

More information is available about global warming political dynamics in the United States than in China. For this reason, I concentrate on the experience of the United States, especially the role special business interests played in preventing the passage of cost-benefit–based climate regulation around carbon taxes and cap and trade. However, since 2006 it is China more than the United States and the EU that has played the bigger emissions role; going forward, it is likely that India and other developing countries will join China in this regard.

---

[5] Before 1989 EU emissions were larger than those from the United States, but the nations currently making up the EU did not constitute a single political entity.

Developing countries can rightly feel that they should not be doubly penalized. They contributed only minimally to cumulative GHG emissions, but disproportionately suffer the impact from past emissions by the developed world, and they ask why they should now be prevented from improving the material living standards of their populations, which lie well below those in the developed world. An important part of climate finance involves investments and wealth transfers from the developed world to developing countries. The magnitude of these investments and transfers will to a large extent be determined in the political arena, and these will be critical for future global emission rates.

1.5 Synopsis

In concluding this section, I note that readers who are interested in a synopsis of what follows can find a short summary in the appendix to this section.

2 Fear Based on Scientific Models of Global Warming

Fear is an emotion that people and animals feel when they sense danger. Fear is typically a response to a stimulus, an alarm warning, suggesting a potential threat.

Typically fear heightens attention to surroundings, inducing a search for threats, an evaluation of the magnitude of potential threats identified, an assessment of possible fight-or-flight responses, and the transmission of an alert to the motor cortex to prepare for an imminent response if necessary.[6]

In this section I describe some of the early scientific work investigating what global warming is and what climate scientists suggested that there is to fear. This discussion will set the stage for future sections about the global community's fight, flight, or freeze response to warnings about global warming.

For behavioral reasons, most of the time I choose to use the phrase "global warming" in place of "climate change." This is because, in 2002, political consultant Frank Luntz recommended the reverse to President Bush, meaning that "climate change" should be used in place of "global warming." Luntz's recommendation was intended to blunt political support for reducing carbon emissions. In a memorandum to the president, Luntz wrote:[7]

> It's time for us to start talking about "climate change" instead of global warming ... "Climate change" is less frightening than "global warming."
> As one focus group participant noted, climate change "sounds like you're

---

[6] Physiologically, fear involves the activation of the amygdala followed by a change in hormonal balance, with an increase in steroid hormones such as adrenalin, cortisol, and testosterone.

[7] Frank Lutz, Memorandum to Bush White House: "The Environment: A Cleaner Safer, Healthier America" (2002). www.sourcewatch.org/images/4/45/LuntzResearch.Memo.pdf.

going from Pittsburgh to Fort Lauderdale." While global warming has cata-strophic connotations attached to it, climate change suggests a more control-lable and less emotional challenge.

Luntz's remarks, especially about "emotional challenge," clearly pertain to the psychology of fear. In this regard, I would highlight two psychological concepts, "framing" and "affect markers," that are relevant to his remarks. "Framing" is a term that psychologists apply to how issues and decision tasks are described, and they emphasize that changes in framing alone can impact the choices people make.[8] "Affect" is a term that psychologists use to describe emotions, positive or negative, and how strong they are.

The reframing of "global warming" as "climate change" was psychologically powerful and contributed to global emissions following a business-as-usual emissions trajectory.

In respect to Luntz's phrase "catastrophic connotations," consider what scientists had been saying about global warming during the prior twenty-five years, beginning with a major report released in 1979.

2.1 The Charney Report, 1979: Cause for Concern

In 1979 the US National Academy of Sciences issued a report entitled "Carbon Dioxide and Climate: A Scientific Assessment." This report came to be called the Charncy report as its team of authors was led by Jule Charney, a highly respected meteorologist from the Massachusetts Institute of Technology.[9] The concern about anthropogenic global warming was not new, but before the Charney report there had been no systematic approach to study it. Moreover, at the time some scientists had proposed an opposing theory – global cooling stemming from anthropogenic aerosol release.[10]

The Charney report was delivered to the Climate Research Board, the Assembly of Mathematical and Physical Sciences, and the National Research Council. Its message to these bodies was stunning and stark. The world had something to fear: growing global warming resulting from high emissions of carbon dioxide into the atmosphere, which occurred when humans burned fossil fuels.

---

[8] Amos Tversky and Daniel Kahneman, "The Framing of Decisions and the Psychology of Choice," *Science* 211(30) (1981), 455–458.

[9] Jule G. Charney, Akio Arakawa, D. James Baker et al., *Carbon Dioxide and Climate: A Scientific Assessment. Report of an Ad Hoc Study Group on Carbon Dioxide and Climate. Woods Hole, Massachusetts, July 23–27, 1979* (Washington, DC: National Academy of Sciences, 1979).

[10] For the history leading up to this report, see Nathaniel Rich, *Losing Earth: A Recent History* (New York: MCD, 2019). Rich also describes the concern about aerosols inducing a new ice age. Jule Charney, the lead author of the report, has been described as the "father of modern meteorology."

The mechanism the Charney report studied is straightforward and relatively easy to describe and can be likened to the way a greenhouse is used to trap heat in order to grow plants. This analogy led to the term "greenhouse effect" being applied to global warming.

Solar radiation passes through the Earth's atmosphere unabsorbed because of its frequency and strikes the Earth's surface, thereby warming it. In turn the heat at the surface results in infrared radiation, which is directed back through the atmosphere. Some of the infrared radiation makes its way into space, but not all, because it has a very different frequency, which can excite the molecules of carbon dioxide and other GHGs. Because of this, a portion is trapped by the atmosphere, thereby adding warmth to the planet. The amount of infrared radiation that is trapped depends on the concentration of carbon dioxide in the atmosphere. The higher the concentration, the warmer the average temperature of the planet.

Contained within the Charney report is the following critical sentence: "We estimate the most probable global warming for a doubling of CO_2 to be near 3°C with a probable error of $\pm$ 1.5°C."

This sentence presents, in quantitative terms, what there is to fear. The technical term for the underlying concept is "climate sensitivity," and it refers to the degree to which the average global temperature of the Earth's atmosphere is sensitive to the atmospheric concentration of carbon dioxide.

As a general matter, global warming can be a good thing. The Earth would be far less hospitable to human existence if the atmosphere were colder because it did not trap infrared radiation. The fear is that the rate of fossil fuel consumption during the industrial age has produced too much of a good thing and therefore we have excessive global warming.[11]

To gain a sense of how atmospheric carbon concentration looked in 1979 when the Charney report was released, consider Figure 1. This figure displays the history of a time series of concentration levels during the past 805,000 years. You will see that, for almost the entire period, concentration levels varied between 200 and 300 parts per million (ppm). Lower concentration levels are associated with ice ages, and higher concentration levels are associated with warming periods. Carbon dioxide ppm in 1979 was 337, having breached the previous 300 "resistance level" in 1914.

---

[11] Our World in Data. https://ourworldindata.org/about. This is why all the work we ever do is made available in its entirety as a public good. Visualizations and text are licensed under CC BY that you may freely use for any purpose. Our data are available for download. All code we write is open-sourced under the MIT license and can be found on GitHub.

Global atmospheric CO₂ concentration

Atmospheric carbon dioxide (CO₂) concentration is measured in parts per million (ppm). Long-term trends in CO₂ concentrations can be measured at high-resolution using preserved air samples from ice cores.

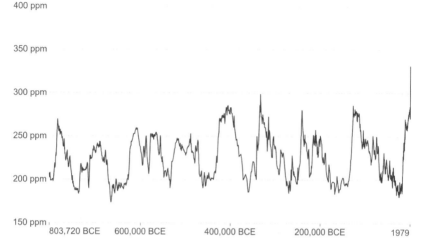

Figure 1 Time series of global atmospheric concentration.
Source: Our World in Data, NOAA, series ending in 1979.

The Charney report was first and foremost a report written by scientists for scientists. The authors of the Charney report were careful in what they wrote. They were clear in stating to what their estimate of 3°C refers and careful to provide a confidence interval to characterize their subjective sense of the precision of their estimate.

The authors of the Charney report were careful to qualify their conclusions, writing:

> In order to address this question in its entirety, one would have to peer into the world of our grandchildren, the world of the twenty-first century. Between now and then, how much fuel will we burn, how many trees will we cut? How will the carbon thus released be distributed between the earth, ocean, and atmosphere? How would a changed climate affect the world society of a generation yet unborn? A complete assessment of all the issues will be a long and difficult task. (pp. vii–viii)

The Charney report asks general questions, but does not focus on specific unfavorable events that might make readers fearful. In particular, the report does not speak about costs, damages, crop loss, deaths, or drought.

The authors of the Charney report were clear about where they were less confident: "At present, we cannot simulate accurately the details of regional climate and thus cannot predict the locations and intensities of regional climate changes with confidence. This situation may be expected to improve gradually as greater scientific understanding is acquired and faster computers are built."

2.2 Hansen, 1981: Equations to Fear

The authors of the Charney report acknowledge assistance provided by James Hansen, who at the time was at the Goddard Institute for Space Studies at the National Aeronautics and Space Administration (NASA). The reason that NASA engaged climate scientists was to study the climate on other bodies in the solar system.

In 1981 Hansen was the lead author on an article entitled "Climate Impact of Increasing Atmospheric Carbon Dioxide" that appeared in the prestigious journal *Science*.[12] This article, which I will call Hansen (1981), is remarkable and quantifies the source of fear about global warming.

Hansen (1981) describes the science of the "greenhouse effect" underlying global warming. The article reviews historical data pertaining to atmospheric carbon dioxide concentration. It uses a series of theoretical models to analyze these data; it discusses impacts on climate from oceans, snow, ice, aerosols, and clouds; it examines the evidence for human-caused global warming; and it offers hypotheses about when the impact of human-induced global warming would become salient.

With more than forty years having passed since the publication of Hansen (1981), it is worth reviewing the article's methodology and hypotheses. Hansen (1981) provided two equations to describe the greenhouse effect. The two equations are

$$S_0 \pi R^2 (1 - A) = 4\pi R^2 \sigma T_e^4, \text{ and}$$

$$T_s = T_e + \Gamma H.$$

These equations have two temperature variables, T_e and T_s. T_e corresponds to there being no greenhouse effect and T_s corresponds to there being a greenhouse effect.

To understand the first equation, think of the Earth as a nearly black disc of radius R with a razor-thin atmosphere that is being struck by energy from the sun. The amount of solar energy per square meter is denoted by S_0. A fraction of the solar radiation, denoted by A and called the "albedo," is

---

[12] James Hansen, David Johnson, Andrew Lacis et al., "Climate Impact of Increasing Atmospheric Carbon Dioxide," *Science* 213(4511) (1981), 957–966.

reflected back up to the sun. The remaining fraction (*1-A*) is absorbed by the disc, which heats up.[13]

The energy associated with the warming of the disc leads to infrared thermal radiation from the Earth's surface rising from the disc. This outgoing infrared radiation is simply a longer wavelength version of the incoming solar radiation. The amount of energy associated with the infrared radiation is $4\pi R^2 \sigma T_e^4$ where T_e denotes the temperature of the disc measured in degrees Kelvin (K) and σ is the Stefan–Boltzmann constant.[14] Notice that there is only one variable in this expression, namely temperature T_e: all the other terms are constants. Therefore, a rise in thermal energy can only come about because of an increase in temperature!

The first of the two GHG equations describes an equilibrium when the amount of infrared energy being radiated from the nearly black disc is equal to the amount of solar energy being absorbed by the disc. When ingoing and outgoing energy are equal, the temperature of the disc remains constant.

Rearranging the first "no greenhouse effect" equation leads to the following expression for the equilibrium temperature:

$$T_e = [S_0(1-A)/4\sigma]^{1/4}.$$

To arrive at a value of T_e via this equation, Hansen (1981) uses as values $A \sim 0.3$ and $S_0 \sim 1367$ watts per square meter. Doing so yields $T_e \sim 255°K$, which is approximately $-18°C$ or $-0.5°F$.

The average surface temperature of the Earth lies above, not below, the freezing temperature of water, and therefore also lies above $-18°C$. Hansen (1981) states that the average surface temperature of the Earth is about $33°K$ higher than $255°K$, and attributes the $33°K$ difference to the greenhouse effect associated with Earth's atmosphere.

Hansen denotes the average temperature of the Earth by T_s with the difference $T_s - T_e$ being $33°K$. In other words, the second GHG equation expresses this difference as ΓH. Here H (for height) represents the relevant height of the atmosphere in kilometers (which Hansen [1981] defines as "H is the flux-weighted mean altitude of the emission to space"). Hansen departs from the assumption of the first equation that the Earth's atmosphere is razor thin (meaning of dimension zero). The other parameter in Hansen's second equation,

---

[13] More generally, this equation includes a variable called emissivity, which appears on the right-hand side as a multiplicand and takes on a value between 0 and 1. Black bodies have an emissivity of 1 while totally reflective bodies, like mirrors, have an emissivity of 0. Hansen (1981) treats the Earth as a black body. On another matter, the power of 4 in the first equation appears to have been inadvertently omitted in the original article.

[14] 0° Kelvin, the temperature associated with zero energy, corresponds to $-273°$Celsius.

Γ (for global warming), is the average rate of temperature increase per kilometer.

Hansen (1981) states that $\Gamma \sim 5°C$ to $6°C$ per kilometer. The greenhouse effect occurs because carbon dioxide in the atmosphere features a "wavelength window," whose width spans 7 to 14 micrometers.

When humans burn fossil fuels and emit carbon dioxide into the atmosphere, they negatively impact the "window," thereby increasing the strength of the greenhouse effect. In theory, emissions cause an increase in Γ, and the increase in Γ causes an increase in T_s, the temperature at the Earth's surface. Hansen (1981) explains that increased "atmospheric CO_2 tends to close this window and cause outgoing radiation to emerge from higher, colder levels, thereby warming the surface and lower atmosphere by the so called greenhouse mechanism" (p. 957).

Hansen (1981) explains the effect using the analogy of a pail. Imagine a pail half filled with water, with a hole at the bottom and a source of incoming water at the top. The hole provides the aforementioned analogy of the carbon dioxide window.

Suppose that the amount of inflow at the top of the pail is the same as the amount of outflow at the bottom, so that the level of water in the pail remains constant. This is a point of equilibrium.

Now suppose that we make the hole at the bottom of the pail a little smaller. This is analogous to adding carbon dioxide to the atmosphere and reducing the width of the carbon dioxide window. Temporarily, the outflow at the bottom of the pail will decrease and the amount of water in the pail will begin to rise. The added weight of the water will increase the amount of pressure in the pail, which in turn will increase the rate of outflow at the bottom. The higher rate of outflow at the bottom is the analogy for a higher surface temperature that results from a narrowing of the window (reduction in the hole at the bottom of the pail).

Hansen (1981) begins by communicating what there is to fear from the burning of fossil fuels. In 1880 atmospheric carbon dioxide lay in the range of 280 to 300 ppm. A hundred years later it lay in the range of 335 to 340 ppm. Besides the burning of fossil fuels, deforestation and changes in biosphere growth also contributed to the higher carbon dioxide concentration.

Hansen (1981) contains several forward-looking hypotheses. First, atmospheric carbon dioxide concentration will reach 600 ppm in the twenty-first century, even if growth of fossil fuel use is slow. Second, and as part of a nested hypothesis, this doubling of carbon dioxide concentration will result in a mean warming of $2°$ to $3.5°C$. Third, natural variability will make it difficult to identify anthropogenic carbon dioxide warming before the end of the twentieth century. Thereafter, signs of global warming will begin to appear, such as droughts in North America and Central Asia, erosion of the West Antarctic Ice Sheet, melting of Arctic ice and opening of the Northwest Passage, and a consequent worldwide rise in sea levels.

For the record, the American Southwest is experiencing a two-decade-long drought. The levels of human-constructed lakes associated with the Colorado River, which is the major source of water for much of this region, are down to approximately one-third of their pre-drought levels. There is a major drought in Central Asia. The West Antarctic Ice Sheet is indeed melting, and Arctic melt is opening the Northwest Passage in summer. Sea levels are rising, albeit slowly.[15]

Keep in mind that Hansen led a group of scientists from NASA, who study climate on other celestial bodies. Hansen (1981) tested greenhouse theory comparing the range of conditions found on Earth, Mars, and Venus. The paper reports:

> [A]tmospheric composition of Mars, Earth, and Venus lead to mean radiating levels of about 1, 6, and 70 km, and lapse rates of $\Gamma \sim 5°$, $5.50°$, and $7°C\ km^{-1}$, respectively. Observed surface temperatures of these planets confirm the existence and order of magnitude of the predicted greenhouse effect. Data now being collected by spacecraft at Venus and Mars will permit more precise analyses of radiative and dynamical mechanisms that affect greenhouse warming. (p. 958)

2.3 Sagan, 1985: Data from Venus to Fear

Carl Sagan was a brilliant astrophysicist on the faculty of Cornell University. In addition to being a productive scholar, he was a prolific author and television personality. Notably, he had once been a proponent of global cooling theory. However, in 1985 he testified before Congress on the topic of global warming. Much of his testimony repeated the messages from the Charney report and Hansen (1981).[16] However, he also spoke about what subsequent research had revealed about the atmosphere of the planet Venus.

Sagan told the committee that Venus is about the same size as Earth, is closer to the sun than Earth, and has a much thicker and brighter cloud cover than does Earth. In particular, he noted that Venus' atmosphere has a much higher concentration of carbon dioxide than Earth's. This is important, he said, because the thicker cloud cover would induce a lower surface temperature on Venus than on Earth, even though Venus is closer to the sun.

---

[15] www.doi.gov/ocl/colorado-river-drought-conditions; https://tinyurl.com/yc6bxaka; https://tinyurl.com/6t9drzsr; https://tinyurl.com/2bna49dr.

[16] See Carl Sagan's 1985 congressional testimony. www.youtube.com/watch?v=3rA8c4sqQJw&t=917s.

Sagan went on to say that, nevertheless, Venus' high atmospheric concentration of carbon dioxide – ninety times greater than that of Earth – offsets the cloud cover effect. This causes a spectacular and extreme greenhouse effect, with the result that the surface temperature on Venus is approximately 470°C, which of course is unsuitable for life as we know it.

The climatic relationships are similar on Mars, Jupiter, and Titan (one of Saturn's moons), in the sense that all have atmospheres and all display some form of greenhouse effect. Importantly, the atmospheres of these bodies are all different in terms of chemical composition and carbon dioxide concentration. Sagan emphasized that it has been possible to calculate these greenhouse effects fairly accurately, and this provides important validation for the applicability of the models climate scientists use.

2.4 Hansen, 1988: Temperature Predictions to Fear

In June 1988 it was James Hansen's turn to generate media headlines by giving testimony before Congress.[17] His remarks foreshadowed findings that he published two months later in an article entitled "Global Climate Changes As Forecast by Goddard Institute for Space Studies Three-Dimensional Model."[18]

Hansen began his testimony by summarizing the three main points he wanted to communicate. First, in 1988 the temperature of Earth was warmer than it had been since instrumental measurements had been taken of temperature. Second, with 99 percent certainty, the higher temperatures are the result of the greenhouse effect. Third, the probability of extreme weather events, such as summer heat waves, is discernably higher because of the impact of fossil fuels on the greenhouse effect.

Hansen (1981) stated that "The global temperature rose by 0.2°C between the middle 1960's and 1980, yielding a warming of 0.4°C in the past century." He was cautious about being able to discern the effects of global warming during the 1980s. His 1988 testimony makes clear he had changed his mind since 1981.

> The observed warming during the past 30 years ... is the period when we have accurate measurements of atmospheric composition ... The warming is almost 0.4 degrees Centigrade by 1987 relative to ... the 30 year mean, 1950 to 1980 and in fact, the warming is more than 0.4 degrees Centigrade in 1988. The probability of a chance warming of that magnitude is about 1 percent. So,

---

[17] For a description of Hansen's political activities during the 1980s, see Nathaniel Rich, "Losing Earth: The Decade We Almost Stopped Climate Change," *New York Times*, August 1, 2018. https://tinyurl.com/86cxpdk4.

[18] James Hansen, Inez Fung, Andrew Lacis et al., "Global Climate Changes As Forecast by Goddard Institute for Space Studies Three-Dimensional Model," *Journal of Geophysical Research* 93(D8) (1988), 9341–9364.

with 99 percent confidence, we can state that the warming during this time period is a real warming trend.

In his testimony Hansen also focused on the American Southeast and Midwest, observing that his group's models suggested high temperatures and low precipitation during the late 1980s and the 1990s. It is significant that for quite some time the Southeast has been experiencing drought conditions.[19]

One of the most important portions of Hansen's testimony was his predicted series for Earth's temperature rise during the subsequent thirty years. Figure 2 displays both the actual time series (thick black line), a confidence interval for actual temperature to reflect measurement error, and three representative scenarios (to the right of the vertical red bar) for the period 1990 through 2020.

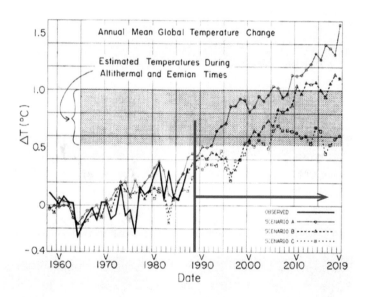

Figure 2 Reference scenario predictions of global temperature change.

Source: "Global Climate Changes As Forecast by Goddard Institute for Space Studies Three-Dimensional Model."

Concentrate on the middle prediction scenario in Figure 2, which Hansen refers to as scenario B. The end point of this scenario reflects an approximate 0.6°C temperature increase during the thirty-year period. Scenario B is Hansen's best guess in 1988 about how the Earth's temperature might evolve

---

[19] See www.drought.gov/dews/southeast. The American Southwest is also in drought. The Colorado River feeds Lake Mead outside of Las Vegas. As of May 31, 2022, Lake Mead was only at 27 percent capacity.

between 1990 and 2020, given a moderate response by humans to the threat of global warming. Scenario A is Hansen's best guess should emission rates between 1990 and 2020 continue at the same rate from 1968 to 1988. Scenario C is Hansen's best guess should emission rates fall drastically between 1990 and 2020.

2.5 Updated Charts and Analysis to Fear

Figure 3 displays actual temperature increases for the period 1880 through 2021, updating the data presented in Figure 2. Figure 3 tells us that scenario B in Figure 2 came closest to the actual trajectory. Notably, in line with scenario B, the actual temperature of Earth did increase by approximately 0.6°C during the thirty-year forecast period 1990–2000. Given the context of Hansen's overall predictions, this is cause for fear.[20]

Figure 4, pertaining to carbon dioxide emissions, updates Figure 1 from 1979 to 2021. The spike in atmospheric concentration at the right, from below 340 to above 410, is cause for fear.

Consider the volume of emissions between 1750 and 1988, the year of Hansen's congressional testimony. Because of exponential growth, it took until just 2017, thirty years, for that volume to double. This might surprise some readers because of a tendency known as exponential growth bias. Exponential growth bias is the tendency to under weight the impact of exponential growth.

Taken together, Figures 3 and 4 provide support for the general contention of the Charney report that the relationship between atmospheric carbon dioxide concentration and the Earth's temperature is positive. Given the data on carbon dioxide emissions and the presence of exponential growth bias, this is cause for fear.

A study published in 2020 updated the climate sensitivity range proposed by the Charney report, which stipulates that a doubling of atmospheric carbon dioxide concentration will lead to a temperature rise between 1.5°C and 4.5°C. The updated range is between 2.6°C and 3.9°C.[21] The increase in the lower bound, from 1.5°C to 2.6°C, is cause for fear.

In 2021 the Intergovernmental Panel on Climate Change (IPCC) released a report that included projections of likely conditions on Earth should the

---

[20] A minority of climate scholars contend that the evidence does not support the conclusion that Hansen's temperature forecast has borne out. See Ross McKitrick and John Christy, "The Hansen Forecasts 30 Years Later." https://tinyurl.com/58tjha3x.

[21] https://tinyurl.com/mr23fxxh. See Steven Sherwood, Mark J. Web, James D. Annan et al., "An Assessment of Earth's Climate Sensitivity Using Multiple Lines of Evidence," *Reviews of Geophysics* 58(4) (2020), e2019RG000678. https://doi.org/10.1029/2019RG000678. The study, conducted by the World Climate Research Programme (WCRP), relied on three types of evidence: trends indicated by contemporary warming, what is known about feedback effects that can modify the rate of climate change, and insights gained from ancient climates.

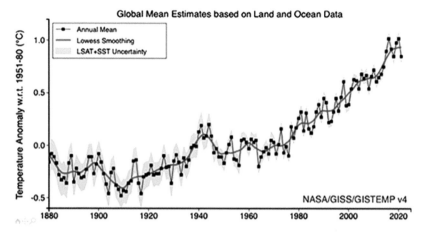

Figure 3 Global mean estimates of Earth's temperature.

Source: NASA. https://tinyurl.com/mtaz3cfv

Global atmospheric CO2 concentration

Atmospheric carbon dioxide (CO_2) concentration is measured in parts per million (ppm). Long-term trends in CO_2 concentrations can be measured at high-resolution using preserved air samples from ice cores.

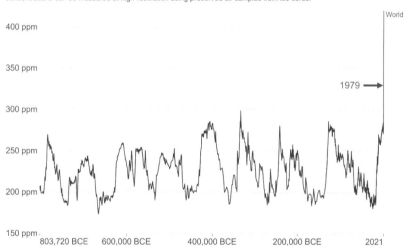

Figure 4 Time series of global atmospheric concentration.

Source: Our World in Data, NOAA, series ending in 2021

temperature rise by 3°C.[22] The projections describe the increased frequency of deadly heat waves, wildfires, and downpours. As ocean temperatures increase, the rise in ocean acidity will devastate fish populations and coral reefs. Mass

---

[22] See *IPCC Sixth Assessment Report: Working Group 1: The Physical Science Basis.* www.ipcc.ch/report/ar6/wg1/#TS.

extinctions will occur. Sea levels will rise, not immediately but ultimately, reshaping entire coastlines.

Psychologically, it can be difficult to visualize what the world will be like if the temperature rises by 3°C. People respond better to narratives than to statistical descriptions. Media coverage of the 2021 IPCC report has tried to help in this regard. For example, *The Economist* ran an article containing a graphic video entitled "This Is what 3°C of Global Warming Looks Like."[23]

Author Nathaniel Rich (2018) provides a characterization of what is to be feared from different degrees of warming.[24] A rise of 2°C would entail the eventual extinction of the world's tropical reefs, an increase of several meters in sea levels, and abandonment of the Persian Gulf. Rich notes that Hansen described 2°C warming as "a prescription for long-term disaster." A rise of 3°C would bring about the emergence of forests in the Arctic and the destruction of most coastal cities. A rise of 4°C would result in Europe being in permanent drought, large areas of China, India, and Bangladesh becoming desert, the Colorado River slowing to a trickle, and the American Southwest becoming mostly uninhabitable. A rise of 5°C holds the serious prospect of human civilization coming to an end.

In 2022 the IPCC released a report that included its most detailed assessment of the threat posed by global warming. The report states that the global community is underinvesting in activities that would protect cities, farms, and coastlines from the hazards associated with global warming, especially droughts and rising sea levels.[25] The 2021 and 2022 assessments issued by the IPCC are cause for fear, and in respect to fight or flight, the message from the IPCC is that the global community needs to be fighting climate change much more vigorously.

The following set of figures provide an indication of why emissions of carbon dioxide are likely to continue globally. Figure 5 provides a comparison of cumulative contributions of carbon dioxide emissions to the atmosphere among several countries. Cumulatively, the United States has been the world's largest emitter of carbon dioxide into the atmosphere.

Figure 6 displays the time series of annual contributions of atmospheric carbon dioxide for the four countries whose data are displayed in Figure 5. Notably, in 2006, annual emissions in the United States peaked and the United

[23] See "This Is What 3°C of Global Warming Looks Like," *The Economist*, October 30, 2021. https://bit.ly/44k2VYq. Also see Zahra Hirji, "The World Is on Track to Warm 3 Degrees Celsius This Century: Here's What That Means," *BuzzFeed*, October 30, 2021. https://bit.ly/3scT0GJ.
[24] Rich, "Losing Earth."
[25] See the *New York Times* coverage of the report: Brad Plumer and Raymond Zhong, "Climate Change Is Harming the Planet Faster Than We Can Adapt, U.N. Warns," *New York Times*, February 28, 2022. https://bit.ly/3KLJyAM.

Annual CO₂ emissions

Carbon dioxide (CO₂) emissions from fossil fuels and industry¹. Land use change is not included.

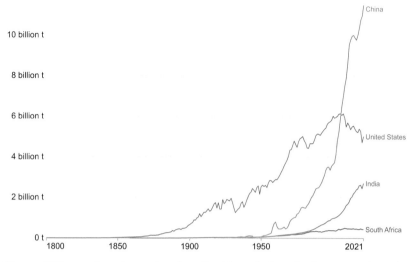

Figure 5 Time series of annual carbon dioxide emissions for four countries – the United States, China, India, and South Africa

Cumulative CO₂ emissions

Cumulative emissions are the running sum of CO₂ emissions produced from fossil fuels and industry¹ since 1750. Land use change is not included.

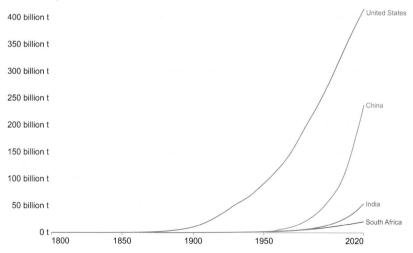

Figure 6 Time series of cumulative carbon dioxide emissions for four countries – the United States, China, India, and South Africa

Annual share of global CO₂ emissions

Carbon dioxide (CO₂) emissions from fossil fuels and industry¹. Land use change is not included.

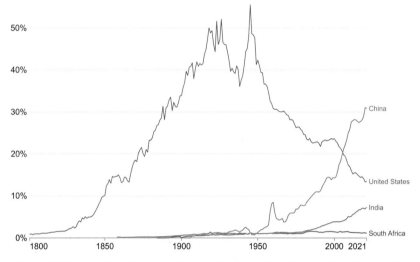

Figure 7 Time series of annual share of carbon dioxide annual emissions for four countries – the United States, China, India, and South Africa

States has reduced annual emissions to its 1986 level. The situation of the EU is similar to that of the United States.

Figure 7, which expresses annual emissions in terms of percentage of contribution, suggests that, going forward, China, India, and the developing world will be the major contributors to carbon dioxide emissions.

Figure 8 compares emissions for the four countries in per capita terms. This figure displays the impact of the drive by developing countries to catch up to developed countries.

For those convinced by climate scientists about the relationship between carbon dioxide emissions and future temperature rise, the emissions momentum from the entire global community, especially developing countries such as China and India, is cause for fear.

2.6 Fear Stemming from the Methane Emergency

Like carbon dioxide, methane is a GHG. In 2021 the IPCC raised a red flag about methane, pointing out that methane emissions have been responsible for about one third of the 1.1°C increase in global temperature since preindustrial times. Moreover, methane emission rates continue to increase, achieving their highest values during the pandemic that began in 2020.[26]

---

[26] See www.youtube.com/watch?v=jraHLXuDFAA.

Per capita CO₂ emissions

Carbon dioxide (CO₂) emissions from fossil fuels and industry¹. Land use change is not included.

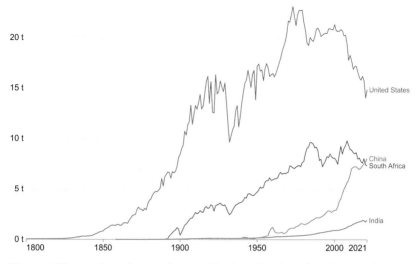

Figure 8 Time series of per capita contribution of carbon dioxide emissions for four countries – the United States, China, India, and South Africa

Over a twenty-year period, methane is more than eighty times as potent a GHG as carbon dioxide. Yet, over a period lasting twenty to thirty years, natural processes break down atmospheric methane into carbon dioxide and water. In contrast, the timescale for breaking down atmospheric carbon dioxide is much longer, at least a century.

Nevertheless, it is important not to be complacent about the threat from methane. The natural process for breaking down atmospheric methane is getting saturated by the higher atmospheric methane concentrations. This is a concern because such saturation will lead to even higher levels of warming. Moreover, pools of methane rose from melting permafrost in Siberia, causing great concern that large amounts of methane might be on the verge of escaping into the atmosphere, which would exacerbate an already alarming situation.

While most of this Element focuses on carbon dioxide, I return to the issue of methane in Section 4 and the appendix to Section 6.

2.7 Key Takeaways

The thirty-year predictions from Hansen (1988) about what global temperatures would be in 2019 have turned out to be accurate. A similar statement holds for the forty-year predictions Hansen (1981) made about drought in North America and Central Asia, the melting of the West Antarctic Ice Sheet, rising sea levels, and the opening of the Northwest Passage in the Arctic. The accuracy of these predictions gives credence to Hansen's perspective. It should also engender a strong sense of fear about what is to come as a result of the rate at which humans burn fossil fuels.

The 2021 report from the IPCC paints an alarming picture of what is to come should the temperature rise by 3°C. Readers need to keep in mind this picture, featuring deadly heat waves, droughts, wildfires, floods, extinction of species, and death of coral reefs. This picture plays a central role in the sections to follow.

While fear is the emotion that triggers a fight-or-flight reaction, there is a third possible response, and that is to freeze, as in "deer in the headlights." The 2022 message from the IPCC is that the global community appears frozen as it stares at the looming threat posed by global warming, and needs to fight. There is no place to flee, even if humans successfully reach Mars. While annual carbon dioxide emissions in the United States and the EU have peaked, they remain high. Of special concern is that emissions continue to rise rapidly in the developing world; this is indeed something to fear.

3 The Nordhaus Integrated Assessment Model

Economists use IAMs to analyze climate policy. An IAM is a microeconomic model in which the production sector reflects the effects of global warming. The effects are bidirectional. Economic activity involves the burning of fossil fuels to create economic output. In turn, the state of the climate impacts the ability of the economy to convert inputs into usable outputs, meaning outputs undamaged by the impact of global warming.[27]

In 2018 William Nordhaus received a Nobel Prize in economics for developing the first IAM to analyze global warming. Nordhaus named his model the Dynamic Integrated Climate-Economy model and refers to it by its acronym, DICE.[28] Notably, he uses DICE to analyze two cases, a base case corresponding to business-as-usual behavior, which I describe in further detail in what follows, and an optimal case corresponding to the maximization of a social planner's objective function.

I devote this section to explaining the structure of DICE, with four objectives in mind.

---

[27] One of the most important features of DICE is that it provides a framework for defining and estimating the social cost of carbon, the basis for arriving at a cost-benefit–based global price of carbon. This issue is discussed in Section 4.

[28] The DICE model is developed in Nordhaus, *Managing the Global Commons*. Elaboration can be found in Nordhaus and Sztorc, *DICE User's Manual*. Information about the 2016 version of the DICE model can be found in Nordhaus, "Revisiting the Social Cost of Carbon."

The first objective is to provide a broad overview of IAMs, the intellectual structure which mainstream economists use to analyze global warming. Here I endeavor to explain how economists think. In the appendix to this section, I discuss the specific structure of DICE.

The second objective pertains to climate finance and how it is embodied within the IAM approach. Climate finance has as its focus investments for mitigating GHG emissions along with their associated financing.

The third objective relates to the nature of public policies to deal with external effects associated with global warming, such as free riding and corresponding market failures. At the heart of these policies is the notion of a suitable "price on carbon." In this respect, DICE is more than a theoretical framework. Nordhaus built DICE in order to inform the combined acts of forecasting the trajectory of climate finance and the setting of climate policy. In the DICE framework, the "price of carbon" governs the degree to which emissions abatement activity varies from the behavioral business-as-usual case.

The fourth objective is to differentiate two sets of results from DICE – those that appear to be consistent with the perspective of mainstream climate scientists, and those that appear to be inconsistent. This is important because there is a tension between mainstream climate scientists' warnings about global warming and the recommendations from DICE about suitable climate policy.[29] I discuss how this tension can be viewed as a continuation of the late twentieth-century debate about population growth between scientist Paul Ehrlich and economist Julian Simon.[30]

The most recent version of DICE dates to 2016, with initial conditions from 2015. I refer to this version of DICE as DICE-2016. Based on DICE-2016, the global carbon price from the behavioral business-as-usual case for the period ending in 2030 is $2.69. According to DICE, this price leads to 3.8 percent of potential emissions being abated at a cost of 0.001 percent of global output. In contrast, in the DICE-2016 optimal case, the figures for 2030 are much higher than the behavioral case: the carbon price is $51.17 and correspondingly 23.7 percent of potential emissions is abated at a cost of 1 percent of output.

In the appendix to this section I discuss how the components of DICE fit together in order to provide a coherent approach to climate finance and carbon pricing. In Section 6 I discuss how other IAMs have been built by modifying and extending DICE. The optimal cases from these IAMs were by and large closer to the perspectives of mainstream climate scientists than the optimal case

---

[29] Mainstream includes the authors of the Charney report, James Hansen, Carl Sagan, and most of the contributors to the IPCC reports.

[30] See Paul Sabin, *The Bet: Paul Ehrlich, Julian Simon, and Our Gamble over Earth's Future* (New Haven, CT: Yale University Press, 2013).

from DICE. However, DICE was the dominant IAM from the 1980s through the first two decades of the current century. Because my aim is to identify key psychological issues in the response to global warming, I focus heavily on DICE for most of the Element. To the extent possible, I want to try and avoid hindsight bias, which is the tendency to look at the past with the unwarranted view that the unfolding of actual events was highly predictable.

In respect to consistency with the perspective of mainstream climate scientists, Nordhaus built DICE so that its assumptions about climate sensitivity and population growth are consistent with the perspectives of mainstream climate scientists. Notably, the behavioral business-as-usual case features the temperature of the Earth increasing above 3°C by the end of the century. This is important, although not especially surprising. Keep in mind from the discussion in Section 2 that the 2021 report from the IPCC paints an alarming picture of what is to come should the global temperature rise by 3°C.

In respect to inconsistency with the perspective of mainstream climate scientists, the optimal case also features the temperature of the Earth increasing above 3°C by the end of the century, with per capita consumption robustly increasing over the course of this century and into the next, despite global warming. This is important, and very surprising to those who share the perspective of mainstream climate scientists.

The inconsistency raises the question of whether Nordhaus' assumptions are excessively optimistic, or whether those of mainstream climate scientists are unduly pessimistic. Optimism and pessimism are psychological biases and will be the subject of future sections. Indeed, the analysis in those sections will build on the framework introduced in the present section.

The state of global warming is very different in the 2020s than it was in 1979. So too is our knowledge of human psychology. However, that psychology is virtually the same today as it was in 1979. The question is whether our increased knowledge of psychology will lead humans to behave more sensibly as they respond to the increased threat posed by global warming.

3.1 Structure of DICE: General Character

Integrated assessment models focus on the manner in which the global economy impacts the climate and vice versa. The bidirectional dynamic involves the economy producing large quantities of industrial emissions of carbon dioxide, which increase future atmospheric temperatures, with the rising temperatures in turn causing major damage to the economy.

Consider the initial conditions for DICE-2016. In 2015 the $105 trillion global economy emitted 38 gross (metric) tons of carbon dioxide into the atmosphere. At the time, the atmospheric temperature was 0.85°C higher than it was in 1750. One estimate of the damage generated as a result of the higher temperature was $0.179 trillion.[31] Decarbonization requires abatement. In 2015 there was some attempt at emission abatement, and the associated cost was $0.001 trillion.

In 2015 the global economy consumed 74 percent of the $105 trillion it produced as output. The remainder went to investment in capital goods, which increased the future productive capacity of the economy.[32] The increased capital, along with a growing population and technical progress, provides the basis for future economic growth and emissions. Future damages from global warming will be a side effect of that growth.

In respect to climate, DICE presents a set of equations to explain the impact of atmospheric carbon concentration on global temperature. Given the Hansen (1981) equation for global temperature, $T_s = T_e + \Gamma H$, DICE explains the temperature transition dynamics associated with changes in Γ resulting from emissions of carbon dioxide. These dynamics involve a carbon cycle in which carbon dioxide exchanges take place among the atmosphere, upper oceans, and deep oceans: temperatures in all three layers are increasing.

The oceans are an important component of the global warming dynamic. Oceans will probably play a key role in humans' attempt to mitigate carbon dioxide emissions, and for that reason alone it is important to include an ocean component in the model.

Notably, the steady state of the DICE climate equations encapsulates the mean climate sensitivity statement from the Charney report – a doubling of carbon dioxide concentration ultimately generates an approximately 3.5°C increase in atmospheric temperature. In respect to the global economy, DICE presents a set of equations to explain the role of carbon dioxide emissions as part of the investment and saving activity that underlie economic growth. The role is bidirectional. The first direction involves carbon dioxide emissions that occur in the act of producing output, and the DICE equations specify how much. The second direction involves the impact of these emissions on the climate, the subsequent increase in global temperature, and the creation of negative feedback in the form of damage to future output. The DICE model incorporates a set of equations to demonstrate the abatement technology required to decarbonize, the cost of the associated abatement, and the degree of climate damage.

The welfare of the current and future generations is impacted by the state of the economy and the climate. The DICE model uses social welfare analysis to

---

[31] One example of a cost would be crop failures from drought.
[32] Capital goods reside in both the private and public sectors of the global economy.

analyze how the global community should evaluate the mitigation of current emissions in order to balance the needs of the present against those of the future.

3.2 The Microeconomic Representation of the Global Economy

In the appendix to this section I present the equations underlying DICE. In this section I describe the microeconomic structure underlying these equations.

To study the economic aspects of global warming, Nordhaus applies a standard microeconomic framework. A production sector, described by a production possibilities frontier (PPF), reflects the state of the Earth's climate and market prices. In this framework profit-maximizing firms make decisions that determine the economy's "location" on the PPF, and with it, climatic conditions on Earth.

In DICE-2016, there is only one type of physical commodity, but it is intertemporal, meaning that consumption of the commodity is time stamped. For example, consider two commodities – consumption at date t and consumption at date $t + 1$. Figure 9 depicts (the projection) of a PPF, relating consumption at two consecutive dates.

At date t, the price of date t consumption will be set to 1, and the price of date $t + 1$ consumption will be a discount factor having the form $1/(1 + \text{rate of interest})$. A positive rate of interest will lead the price of date $t + 1$ consumption to be less than *1*. The higher the interest rate, the cheaper will be date $t + 1$ consumption relative to date t consumption. Remember that profit-maximizing firms will tilt production toward higher-priced commodities, which means that the production sector invests in order to increase future production when interest rates are relatively low.

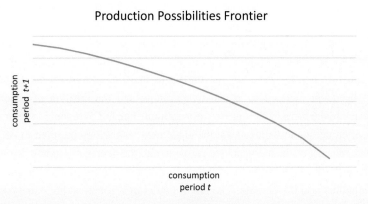

Figure 9 Graph of a production possibilities frontier. The horizontal axis represents quantity of consumption at date t and the vertical axis represents quantity of consumption at date $t + 1$.

I should mention that the PPF displayed in Figure 9 implicitly assumes that capital stock can be consumed just like output. If capital is nonconsumable and can only decrease through depreciation, then consumption at date 2 will have a positive lower bound rather than a zero lower bound.

3.3 The General Character of the DICE-Optimal Solution

The main purpose of DICE is to provide insight about the character of a cost-benefit–based climate finance strategy for the global economy. Nordhaus does so by identifying an optimal solution for the DICE model, which involves maximizing a social welfare function subject to production constraints for the global economy. In the model social welfare is utilitarian, and the production constraints describe how the productive capabilities of the economy and the climate coevolve over time.[33]

Figure 10 is a typical microeconomic chart displaying the character of the optimal solution. The axes in Figure 10 are consumption in the five-year period ending in 2020 (horizontal axis) and consumption in the five-year period ending in 2025 (vertical axis). More generally, DICE models the trade-offs between present and future generations, not just the same generation in successive periods. However, for the purpose of exposition, I focus on successive periods for now.

In the model decisions about consumption, savings, capital accumulation, and emissions abatement lead to movements along the PPF. Each point along the PPF leads to a level of social utility. Finding the optimal solution entails finding the point along the PPF that is associated with the highest social welfare indifference curve. This optimal solution lies at the point of tangency between the PPF and the highest achievable indifference curve.

In DICE each time period consists of five years, with the date label connoting the fifth year of the period. For example, period 2020 comprises the years 2016 through 2020. In the discussion that follows, the term "period" will often be understood.

The slope of the PPF is called the marginal rate of transformation (MRT). This slope measures the ability of the economy to increase total consumption in 2025, meaning period 2025, by foregoing one ton of total consumption in 2020, meaning period 2020. The MRT is the number of tons of 2025-consumption that are "transformed" from one ton of 2020-consumption.

---

[33] At its heart DICE is neoclassical. The following discussion pertains to any neoclassical-based IAM, not just DICE.

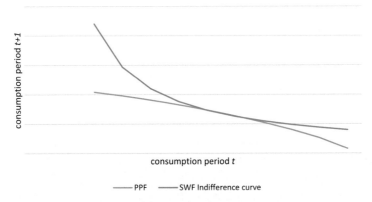

Figure 10 Graph of production possibilities frontier, indifference curve for social welfare function, and tangency between them. The horizontal axis represents quantity of consumption during the five-year period ending in 2020 and the vertical axis represents quantity of consumption during the five-year period ending in 2025.

In DICE-2016 there are two ways to transform 2020-consumption into 2025-consumption. The first is by diverting 2020-output from consumption to capital, thereby increasing the amount of capital in 2025. The second is by engaging in the abatement of emissions that enter the atmosphere in 2020 and incurring the associated costs (in 2020). One example of an abatement activity is the use of a low-emission renewable energy source, which has a higher cost than fossil fuels. A second example is the application of costly carbon capture and sequestration, capturing carbon at its source and sequestering it in the ground so that it does not enter the atmosphere.

Diverting one unit of 2020-output from consumption into capital allows for transfer of one unit of output from period 2020 to period 2025. This additional capital increases productive capacity in period 2025. Suppose that at the DICE-optimum, the extra capital allows 0.87 additional units of output to be produced in 2025 – that is, the marginal productivity of capital (MPK) is 0.87. In DICE-2016 the annual rate of depreciation is 10 percent, which translates into a five-year compounded rate of 61 percent. Therefore, 39 percent (=1–0.61) units of the capital transferred from 2020 to 2025 remain at the end of 2025.[34]

Assuming that capital goods can be consumed if desired, this means that total consumption at the end of 2025 can increase by the sum of 0.39 and 0.87, or 1.26 units. That is, the MRT from 2020-consumption to 2025-consumption is 1.26,

---

[34] The figures used in this numerical illustration are consistent with the parameter values in DICE-2016.

spread out over five years. Of course, if the net capital transfer of 0.39 and MPK of 0.87 are totally consumed, then the extra savings in 2020 will only impact the 2025 period, but not periods after 2025.

The second way to transform 2020-consumption into 2025-consumption is abatement. This means increasing the abatement level in 2020, using resources that would otherwise have produced a single unit of 2020-usable consumption. The reduced emissions of carbon dioxide in 2020 will result in lower temperatures than otherwise in the period 2025 and thereafter. Lower temperatures lead to lower damages, and therefore more undamaged output available for future consumption.

In Figure 10 the point of tangency represents the optimal condition in which the MRT coincides in value with the social marginal rate of substitution (MRS). In the context of Figure 10 the MRS measures how many units of additional 2025-consumption will provide exact compensation "to the social planner" for reducing 2020-consumption by exactly one unit.

At the point of tangency, the MRS and MRT are equal in value. For intertemporal maximization, this equality is known as an "Euler condition." In the example just provided the MRS will be 1.26 because 1.26 is the value of the MRT.

The MRS measures the amount of 2025-consumption required in compensation. The MRT measures how much 2025-consumption the production sector can produce as compensation. At a point on the PPF where MRS > MRT in absolute value, the social planner has over-transformed 2020-consumption into 2025-consumption and requires more 2025-consumption compensation to continue the transformation than the production sector provides. This will lead a maximizing social planner to reverse the transformation. At a point on the PPF where MRS < MRT, the reverse holds.

In respect to carbon capture, you can think of another type of MRT_{2025}, interpreted as the number of additional units of 2025-consumption made available by spending one more unit of 2020-output on abatement. Because abatement in 2020 will also impact 2025-consumption, 2030-consumption, and so on, there will be a sequence of these MRT values: MRT_{2025}, MRT_{2030}, MRT_{2035}, . . .

The aforementioned inverse of MRS, which I will now write as $1/MRS_{2025}$, measures the number of 2020-units the social planner is willing to forego in order to consume one more unit of 2025-consumption. The ratio MRT_{2025} / MRS_{2020} measures the amount of 2020-consumption the social planner would forego in order to consume MRT_{2025} units of 2025-consumption. In this respect, keep in mind that equilibrium discount factors are given by the inverse-MRS values.

Because additional abatement activity in 2020 generates impacts in 2025, 2030, 2035, . . . the sum of ratios,

$$(MRT_{2025}/MRS_{2025}) + (MRT_{2030}/MRS_{2030}) + (MRT_{2035}/MRS_{2035}) + \ldots,$$

measures the total 2020-consumption the social planner would forego in order to experience the additional future consumption stream MRT_{2025}, MRT_{2030}, MRT_{2035}, ...

Of course, what the social planner would forego in 2020 is exactly one unit. Therefore, the optimality condition associated with abatement is:

$$1 = (MRT_{2025}/MRS_{2025}) + (MRT_{2030}/MRS_{2030})$$
$$+ (MRT_{2035}/MRS_{2035}) + \ldots.$$

3.4 Competitive Equilibrium and Climate Finance

In a perfectly competitive economy, the social planner's optimum can be implemented as an equilibrium. Figure 11 illustrates how this is accomplished.

Figure 11 adds a tangency line called the "price line" to Figure 10. The slope of this line is the negative of the price of 2020-consumption relative to 2025-consumption. Because this is an intertemporal problem, the relative price of 2020-consumption is the gross 2020 interest rate. In this model, the interest rate refers to the rate of return on capital, as opposed to the risk-free rate.

Denote the net interest rate by the symbol r. A lower interest rate reduces the incentive to save during 2020, leading to higher 2020-consumption than is the case when the interest rate is higher.

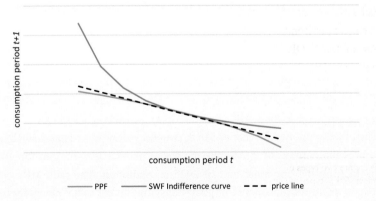

Figure 11 Graph of production possibilities frontier, indifference curve for social welfare function, the tangency between them, and the tangent line whose slope is the negative of relative prices. The horizontal axis represents quantity of consumption during the five-year period ending in 2020 and the vertical axis represents quantity of consumption during the five-year period ending in 2025.

As I discussed earlier, the value of the 2020 gross interest rate coincides with the MRT. In the numerical illustration, the value of the MRT is 1.26. Because a time period covers five years, the associated implied annual interest rate is 5 percent. This is a production side view of how DICE generates values for the return on capital. The demand side view is discussed in Section 4.

From the perspective of consumers, the price line represents a budget constraint, whose slope is determined by the interest rate. Consumers maximize utility subject to being on the budget constraint. The budget constraint is intertemporal and so consumers' decisions pertain to choosing, for any period, how much to consume and how much to save.

Because of population growth, I like to think of a consumer as a family household whose dynamic planning reflects expectations about offspring. This feature is important in order that household preference maps be consistent with those of the social planner.

From the perspective of the production sector, the price line is an iso-value line. Firms maximize value by choosing projects with the highest net present value (NPV) subject to being on the PPF. Some projects involve investments in 2020 capital, and future cash flows occurring in 2025, with the latter discounted using the 2020 interest rate. Other projects involve abatement, for example with firms choosing to increase carbon capture activities in 2020 in order to receive future benefits, which are discounted using the interest rates implied by the 1/MRS ratios.

3.5 How Climate Finance Is Embodied within DICE

Nordhaus built DICE so that its equations for the economy would represent the broad activities of consumption, saving, investment, and growth, all of which occur in an environment featuring global warming.

As an IAM, DICE is a climate economics model. Two of the decision variables in DICE are investment and saving.[35] Both variables reflect the time value of money, which is one of the basic elements of finance.[36] Because both investment and saving in DICE reflect the impact of global warming, DICE also provides a rudimentary framework for climate finance.

---

[35] There are two types of control variables in DICE, one for saving rates and the other for carbon prices. Other types of decision variables, such as for investment and abatement, are determined within DICE by behavioral equations that reflect first-order optimizing conditions.

[36] Because DICE is a certainty model, I do not discuss risk in this section, but do so in Section 6. For a literature review of climate finance with risk, see Alessio Venturini, "Climate Change, Risk Factors and Stock Returns: A Review of the Literature," *International Review of Financial Analysis* 79(C) (2022), https://doi.org/10.1016/j.irfa.2021.101934. In respect to green bonds, see Malcolm Baker, Daniel Bergstresser, George Serafeim, and Jeffrey Wurgler, "Financing the Response to Climate Change: The Pricing and Ownership of U.S. Green Bonds," NBER Working Paper 25194, 2018. www.nber.org/papers/w25194.

In respect to investment, firms that are considering the adoption of a project employ the usual capital budgeting approach based on NPV. Managers of firms ask whether the NPV of the expected project cash flows are nonnegative. If the answer is yes, the project will generate at least a competitive rate of return and can therefore be adopted.

Formally, the NPV question to be answered is whether or not

$$NPV = -CF_0 + CF_1/(1+r_1) + CF_2/(1+r_2)^2 + CF_3/(1+r_2)^3$$
$$+ \ldots \geq 0,$$

where CF_t is the project cash flow at date t, and r_t is the rate of interest prevailing at date t. If the answer is yes, then the project is adopted. Otherwise it is rejected.

In respect to savings, consumers consider a proposed level of savings and ask whether that level is too low, too high, or just right. Then focus on two successive periods, 1 and 2. To ascertain whether the answer is too low, they ask whether the reward to saving provided by the market, which is the gross interest rate, is at least as large as the minimum reward they require. In formal terms, the marginal reward required is the MRS, the amount of period 2 consumption needed to compensate for the reduction of a single unit of period 1 consumption. In other words, the question to be answered is whether or not

$$(1+r_1) \geq MRS.$$

If the answer is yes, then the decision should be to save more, but stopping when $(1+r_1)$ and the MRS are equal, and reducing saving when the inequality goes in the other direction. Notice that the discount factor $1/(1+r_1)$ is given by the inverse-MRS.

The preceding inequality pertains to a comparison between successive periods. In contrast, the equation for NPV pertains to a sequence of periods. Notably, in equilibrium, the discount factors in the preceding equation for NPV are given by the sequence of respective inverse-MRS values.[37]

Most of the investment projects in the economy are conventional and pertain to such things as real estate, roads, bridges, information technology, automobiles, and transportation. However, some projects pertain to global warming, involving investment in alternative energy, carbon capture, and the like.

In theory, the same NPV-based analysis applies to climate projects as conventional projects. There is an initial cash outflow CF_0, and subsequent future cash flows, some of which are positive. The most important future cash flows

---

[37] A typical MRS in this sequence connotes the amount of period t consumption required to compensate for the reduction of a unit of consumption in period 0.

reflect the benefits of reducing climate damages that would otherwise have occurred without the investment.

In equilibrium, interest rates serve to equate the demand for funds to finance projects with the funds generated from savings. Here projects mean all projects, meaning both conventional and climate-related. It is for this reason that interest rates play a critical role in DICE, and for that matter climate finance.

3.6 Pricing Carbon at Its Social Cost

If the production sector of the economy consisted of a single firm, then firm managers would choose the abatement trajectory to maximize the value of the entire production sector. Specifically, the value of all damages associated with emissions would be internalized within the firm. However, when the production sector consists of many firms, then each firm will be naturally inclined to consider the impact of its emissions only on its own profitability, and ignore the external impact on other agents. In this case there is a market failure stemming from an emissions-generated externality. The impact of such a market failure is for insufficient abatement in the aggregate resulting in total carbon dioxide emissions that are too high.

To address market failures involving externalities, economists generally suggest placing "Pigouvian prices" on the sources of the externality. In the case of carbon dioxide emissions, this means pricing carbon dioxide at its social cost – for example, by imposing a tax.

In DICE-2016 Nordhaus computes the optimal case and measures the social cost of carbon dioxide in a given period as the amount of (gross) output that needs to be forgone during that period in order to reduce carbon dioxide emissions by one ton. By focusing on the optimal case, Nordhaus exploits the fact that the social cost of carbon will equal its social benefits. This is why DICE sets the "price" of a ton of carbon dioxide using a formula for its social cost. See the appendix to this section for a formal derivation.

3.7 The Climate-Policy Ramp

An increasing sequence of carbon prices (per ton) over time is generated by DICE-16: \$35 in 2020, \$51 in 2030, \$91 in 2050, \$165 in 2075, and \$271 in 2100. Nordhaus calls this increasing pattern the "climate-policy ramp."

The abatement technology in DICE encompasses the entire process of emission mitigation, such as renewable energy, carbon capture, and transition to electric vehicles. With this in mind, consider how Nordhaus (2007) explains the driver of the climate-policy ramp.[38]

---

[38] William Nordhaus, "The *Stern Review on the Economics of Climate Change*," Working Paper, Yale University, May 3, 2007.

In a world where capital is productive, the highest-return investments today are primarily in tangible, technological, and human capital, including research and development on low-carbon technologies. In the coming decades, damages are predicted to rise relative to output. As that occurs, it becomes efficient to shift investments toward more intensive emissions reductions. The exact mix and timing of emissions reductions depends upon details of costs, damages, and the extent to which climate change and damages are non-linear and irreversible.

As I will discuss in Sections 4 and 5, whether or not the optimal case features a climate-policy ramp is an important issue in IAMs.

Figures 12 and 13 illustrate the climate-ramp pattern for the social cost of carbon, the emissions control rate, and the cost of abatement as a fraction of output.[39] For all three variables, the ramp period pertains to 2015 through 2100.

The jagged segments in Figure 12 are caused by Nordhaus' assumption about the earliest period that carbon emissions can become net negative, which is 2160. This means that once carbon emissions become net zero, they are constrained by a ceiling until 2160, at which time a jump to a higher plateau becomes possible. Nordhaus makes a simplistic assumption that emissions, if net negative, will decline at the rate of 20 percent, corresponding to an emissions control rate of 120 percent.

Net zero and net negative emissions are important issues that are the subject of discussion in subsequent sections. The jagged segments in Figure 12, while unrealistic, reflect important features that I will discuss at length, especially in Section 6.

Nordhaus makes an important assertion about research and development (R&D) in low-carbon technologies:

> [I]t is critical to have a harmonized carbon tax or the equivalent both to provide incentives to individual firms and households and to stimulate research and development in low-carbon technologies. Carbon prices must be raised to transmit the social costs of GHG emissions to the everyday decisions of billions of firms and people.[40]

---

[39] In the appendices, the symbol for the emissions control rate is $\mu(t)$ and the symbol for the cost of abatement as a fraction of output is $\Lambda(t)$.

[40] In respect to the assertion about R&D, I need to point out that formally within DICE, there is no specific capital associated with low-carbon technologies. Instead the model only provides for an abatement technology that is time-varying but otherwise independent of investment activity. When reading Section A3.2.2, readers can verify this point by focusing on the equations relating industrial emissions $E_{Ind}(t)$, abatement activity $\mu(t)$, and abatement unit cost $\Lambda(t)$. Therefore, the point Nordhaus makes about R&D is more a loose interpretation of his model rather than a formal implication. This point is made in Martin C. Hänsel, Moritz A. Drupp, Daniel J. A. Johansson et al., "Climate Economics Support for the UN Climate Targets," *Nature Climate Change* 10, 781–789. www.nature.com/natureclimatechange.

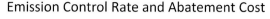

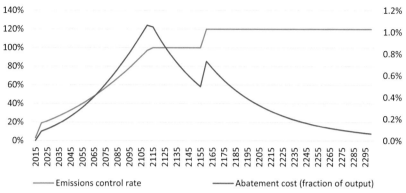

Figure 12 Optimal DICE-2016 trajectories for emission control rate and abatement cost for the period 2015–2300

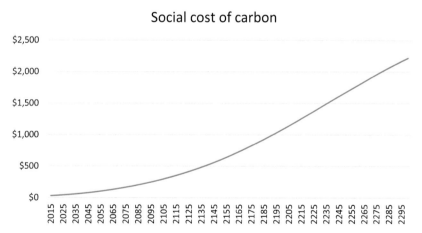

Figure 13 Optimal DICE-2016 trajectory for social cost of carbon for the period 2015–2300

The statement is important and stands in marked contrast to the fact that for the past four decades, the global emissions trajectory has been much closer to the behavioral business-as-usual case than Nordhaus' optimal case.

3.8 Free Riders and Carbon Clubs

As I mentioned earlier, in the absence of Pigouvian prices for carbon dioxide emissions, firms making decisions based only on their own private interests will engage in excessive emissions relative to the optimum. Expressed differently, in the absence of Pigouvian prices for carbon dioxide emissions, carbon dioxide will be priced below its social cost, abatement will be insufficient, and the resulting equilibrium will be Pareto-inefficient.

A key feature of this type of inefficiency is that one economic agent will benefit from the abatement activities of others, but will not contribute to the costs borne by others. This reluctance is known as "free riding."

Achieving a global Pigouvian pricing structure is especially challenging when firms are distributed geographically across different countries. Nordhaus developed a version of DICE, which he calls C-DICE, to analyze the issues that arise when countries seek to negotiate emissions agreements.[41] I describe the structure of C-DICE in the appendix to this section.

The foundation for C-DICE is based on the economic theory of clubs and cooperative game theory. Economist and Nobel laureate James Buchanan developed the theory of clubs because he was dissatisfied with the use of a social welfare function to analyze the provision of public goods.[42] Economists often treat the theory of public goods as a special case of the theory of externalities.

Economist and Nobel laureate Paul Samuelson introduced the social welfare function technique to the economics literature. In Samuelson's framework, a social planner selects an allocation so that at the margin, the willingness of a community to sacrifice private consumption in order to increase the provision of a public good by a single unit would coincide with the MRT of doing so. Notably, the willingness of a community to sacrifice private consumption is given by the sum of individual MRS values.

Samuelson's theory uses a tax system featuring a single tax rate associated with the public good along with a system of lump sum redistributive wealth transfers. The combination is important because a common tax rate generally implies that some individuals will pay for public goods at a rate that exceeds their corresponding MRS, and some will pay at a rate that is below their corresponding MRS.

Buchanan objected to the idea that people would pay for public goods at prices that differed from their individual MRS values. He regarded such a situation as coercion, and for this reason he rejected the idea of using a social welfare function as the basis of public policy. He suggested focusing instead on market arrangements that would enable people to come together voluntarily in groups. He called these groups "clubs." The main idea of a club is

[41] William Nordhaus, "Climate Clubs: Overcoming Free-Riding in International Climate Policy," *American Economic Review* 105(4) (2015), 1339–1370.
[42] Alain Marciano, "James Buchanan: Clubs and Alternative Welfare Economics," *Journal of Economic Perspectives* 35(3) (2021), 243–256.

that its members share the public good, choose a membership fee structure that allows for variation across individual members, and can exclude potential free riders.

The C-DICE concept combines the idea of a club with the social cost of carbon derived from DICE. Nordhaus built C-DICE to analyze how different countries might form carbon clubs in order to price carbon dioxide emissions at their respective social costs.

Because carbon dioxide emissions are universal and impact everyone, an efficient outcome requires a single global price of carbon and therefore a single club. In game theoretic terms, the club would consist of the "grand coalition" of all nations. This would entail the terms of membership being structured so that no nation judged that it would be better off leaving the grand coalition to join another coalition, including a club consisting of just one member. If such terms can be structured, the grand coalition is said to be stable.

Nordhaus contends that developing the membership terms that would lead to a stable grand coalition is a delicate exercise that needs to be accomplished "top down with external incentives" as opposed to "bottom up with only internal incentives." Here is the argument he makes for why the "bottom up" approach will fail.

Consider an initial case in which there are no carbon clubs and no coordinated carbon price. Each country instead chooses its own price for carbon, taking account of the carbon prices and emissions of other countries. In the context of C-DICE, Nordhaus provides a formal argument to establish that the resulting equilibrium prices for carbon will be approximately 12 percent of its social cost. This equilibrium, which is noncooperative, corresponds to behavioral business as usual.

Nordhaus' conclusion requires emphasis. In the case of business-as-usual, carbon dioxide is actually priced at less than 12 percent of its corresponding social cost. Notably, the carbon price associated with Nordhaus' behavioral business-as-usual case is approximately 6 percent in 2020, declines to 4 percent in 2100, and then gradually rises to 100 percent in 2240.

With the noncooperative equilibrium as starting point, consider what happens when two countries decide to form a carbon club and agree to set a common club price for carbon that is much higher than the prior equilibrium price. Doing so leads the two club members to reduce their joint emissions, thereby benefiting themselves as well as all other countries. The other countries will receive a windfall without any sacrifice on their part. As a result, they will be free riders, even outside of the club.

Keep in mind why the two club members choose to reduce their emissions. They do so because both take account of the impact of their individual contributions on both club members, not just on themselves. For this reason, adding members to a club will reduce individual emission levels for each member and correspondingly raise the uniform club price of carbon.

With this last point in mind, let the two members invite others to join their club, under the condition that any new member agrees to increase its price for carbon to the club level. This invitation will induce the other members to engage in a cost-benefit analysis. Once they join the club, they will no longer be able to free ride.

Will paying the membership fee – meaning setting a higher price for carbon – generate sufficient incremental benefits to offset the value of being free riders on the two-member club? In the context of C-DICE, Nordhaus argues not and concludes that the bottom-up approach will not work. Increasing club size leads the cost of membership to go up for all members, but especially new members who had been free riding. In addition, the benefits of continuing to free ride increase if other members join the club and reduce their emissions as a condition of entry.

All of this leads Nordhaus to propose a top-down process with external incentives for building a stable grand coalition. The top-down feature is similar to the structure used to produce major international agreements such as Bretton Woods, the World Trade Organization, or the World Food Programme.[43] It uses a series of conferences and negotiations, with all parties present, to hammer out the terms.

The external incentives component pertains to elements not related directly to carbon pricing and abatement. Nordhaus suggests structuring a carbon club that uses trade barriers such as tariffs to penalize trading partners who set carbon prices that are lower than those set by club members. Most importantly, he argues that carbon prices, rather than emission quantities, be used as the behavioral variable defining the inclusion/exclusion criteria for club membership.[44] His analysis establishes conditions under which a 2 percent tariff policy would produce a stable grand coalition with a uniform price for carbon that is equal to its social cost. Notably, the conditions involve an upper limit on the price of carbon. Nordhaus argues that the social cost of carbon associated with DICE-2016 is consistent with the emergence of a stable grand coalition.

Recall Buchanan's point about a uniform tax leading some people to pay at a rate that differs from their corresponding MRS. In the Samuelson scheme, this issue is dealt with by lump sum wealth transfers. The same point applies to a uniform price for carbon.

---

[43] I have a personal connection to the negotiations that produced the World Food Programme. See https://tinyurl.com/bddf6zhm.

[44] The appendix to this section contains a quote from Nordhaus on this point.

3.9 Comparing Business-As-Usual and Optimal Cases

I call Nordhaus' base case "behavioral business-as-usual." Nordhaus describes his base case as "baseline" with "no controls," explaining that the term refers to no steps having been taken either to curtail GHG emissions or to internalize the associated externality. In his various writings, he applied the terms "base case" and "baseline" to describe the policy most nations followed through the date of his respective writings.

Nordhaus defines his optimal case as the solution to an optimization problem in which the trajectories for the savings rates and price of carbon (dioxide) maximize a utilitarian social welfare function.

Consider how the two DICE-2016 cases – behavioral business-as-usual and optimal – compare to each other. I do so for the years 2030, 2050, and 2100 and highlight some of the findings in Table 1. There are some surprises.

Table 1 displays the comparison for five indices: atmospheric carbon concentration, atmospheric temperature, the cost of abatement (measured as a fraction of total output), total damage from global warming (measured as a fraction of output), and consumption per capita.

Notice in Table 1 that carbon concentration, atmospheric temperature, and damage from global warming all increase over time, but are lower in the optimal case than in the behavioral case.

The DICE-2016 model predicts that even in the optimal case, atmospheric carbon concentration surpasses 600 by the year 2100. Not to put too fine a point on it, but 600 is double the 300 ppm level discussed in Section 2. Moreover, this is just what Hansen (1981) warned about – reaching 600 ppm in the twenty-first century was virtually inevitable. As for the behavioral case, it features predicted atmospheric concentration in 2100 that is above 800!

Given its prediction for carbon concentration, and consistent with the analysis in the Charney Report, DICE-2016 predicts an atmospheric temperature increase of 3.5°C in 2100 for the optimal case. For the behavioral case, the 2100 prediction is a 4.1°C increase.

Not surprising, the predicted cost of abatement is higher in the optimal case than the behavioral case. The damage from global warming rises steadily over time, but is lower in the optimal case than in the behavioral case. Consumption per capita is higher in the behavioral business-as-usual case than the optimal case for the periods ending in 2030 and 2050, but is lower in 2100.

I believe many readers will be surprised to learn that in all periods, the difference in consumption per capita between the two cases is small, in the

Table 1 Comparison of select variables from DICE-2016: Behavioral business-as-usual case versus optimal case

	2030	2050	2100
Atmospheric concentration of carbon (ppm)			
Behavioral case	459	552	826
Optimal case	451	517	628
Atmospheric temperature (degrees Celsius above preindustrial)			
Behavioral case	1.4	2.1	4.1
Optimal case	1.4	2.0	3.5
Abatement cost (fraction of output)			
Behavioral case	0.001%	0.002%	0.005%
Optimal case	0.131%	0.264%	0.889%
Total damage (fraction of gross output)			
Behavioral case	0.442%	1.068%	3.975%
Optimal case	0.432%	0.976%	2.864%
Consumption per capita ($thous per year)			
Behavioral case	14.89	22.58	52.05
Optimal case	14.86	22.52	52.22

region of 0.2 percent to 0.3 percent, plus or minus. In both cases, predicted consumption per capita is far greater in 2100 than in 2030. The predicted damage from climate change, while rising over time, is not dramatic. In 2100 the magnitude of the damage is under 3 percent for the optimal case and about 4 percent for the behavioral business-as-usual case.

The increase in per capita consumption, according to DICE-2016, occurs from adaptation, as a result of global investment in capital and technology. In this respect, DICE-2016 predicts that per capita consumption increases dramatically during the twenty-first century despite the effects of global warming.

3.10 Debates about Technological Progress and the Shape of the Future

The tension between the perspective of climate scientists described in Section 2 and the perspective provided by DICE-2016 described in Section 3 is of fundamental importance. This tension includes several issues, with the central issue involving the shape of a global warming future.

Climate scientists warn of catastrophic long-term change and climate tipping points associated with global temperature increases above 2°C relative to preindustrial times. In contrast, DICE-2016 predicts significantly higher per capita consumption as the global temperature increase reaches 2°C and rises beyond, even higher than 3.5°C.

The divergent visions of what a global warming future will look like for humans reflects past debates about humans' ability to adapt to changing environments. These debates trace back to the stark warnings Thomas Malthus issued that scarce resources would limit the early gains from the industrial revolution.[45]

Although subsequent history did not support Malthus' warnings, the fears prompted by his concerns continue into the present. One of the most prominent modern debates with a Malthusian theme involved scientist Paul Ehrlich and economist Julian Simon.

During the 1960s Ehrlich advanced the argument that human population growth was far too high and in a matter of decades would generate a series of major disasters. He made this argument in a book he entitled *The Population Bomb*, suggesting that hundreds of millions of people would starve to death in the 1970s and 1980s.[46] The thrust of his argument was that high population growth would outstrip resources, forcing a major decline in per capita consumption.

Simon argued that if Ehrlich were correct, then the increased scarcity of raw materials would lead the relative price of these materials to increase over time. He suggested instead that the global economy would respond to short-term scarcity with the response exerting downward pressure on commodity prices.

In 1980 Simon sharpened the difference of opinion by proposing a wager, a bet if you will. The amount of the bet was $10,000, with the outcome determined by whether the prices of a specific set of commodities, agreed upon by the betting parties, would rise or fall between 1980 and 1990.

Simon won the bet, as all commodities that were part of the wager declined over time. More generally, an agricultural revolution during the 1970s led to an improvement in living standards, not the mass starvation Ehrlich predicted. When Ehrlich published his book, about one in four people on Earth did not have enough food to eat. That figure subsequently decreased to one in ten.

---

[45] See www.britannica.com/biography/Thomas-Malthus.

[46] Paul R. Ehrlich, *The Population Bomb* (New York: Ballantine Books, 1968). Ehrlich received much media attention for his perspective. Among his comments was that it would not surprise him if England no longer existed as a country by the year 2000.

In 1990 Ehrlich hoped for a rematch with Simon; Ehrlich wanted the rematch to be about increases in future global temperatures. Unfortunately, Simon died in 1996 before the terms of a rematch could be negotiated.

As I discussed in Section 2, global temperatures did discernably increase after 1995. Perhaps Ehrlich would have won the rematch. Yet I suggest that the increase would not have removed the fundamental tension because this tension pertains to whether standards of living will increase despite the rise in global temperature.[47]

A very insightful book by Hans Rosling was published in 2018: *Factfulness: Ten Reasons We're Wrong about the World: And Why Things Are Better Than You Think.*[48] This title conveys a message, namely that the world suffers from "pessimism bias." Pessimism bias entails the assignment of excessively high probabilities to unfavorable events and correspondingly excessively low probabilities to favorable events.

Rosling tells us that most people are unaware of just how much better human life has become in recent decades. He describes the situation as "mass ignorance" and says he wrote his book in an effort to reverse this state of affairs. Among the many ways Rosling tells us things are better than we believe are the following: cheaper solar panels, a sharp decline in the number of people who are malnourished, increased cereal yields, increased access to the Internet, less poverty, lower infant mortality, fewer battlefield deaths, and fewer plane crashes.

Rosling has a psychological explanation for why pessimism bias persists despite the availability of ample information to the contrary. His explanation involves a "worldview" heavily influenced by dramatic problems from the past, coupled with "confirmation bias," the tendency to overweight evidence that serves to confirm a position we hold and to under weight evidence that is disconfirming. In other words, people begin with views defined by significant social problems and then ignore new information about associated improvements.

To this I would add that if the data Rosling was focusing upon were accessible, but not part of people's memories, then "availability bias" would amplify the pessimism. Availability bias is the tendency to over weight information that is readily available in people's memory relative to information that is not.

Consider what Rosling has to say about climate change. First, he tells us that most people, when responding to surveys, are aware that experts believe that the

---

[47] See Kenneth Arrow, Partha Dasgupta, Lawrence Goulder et al., "Are We Consuming Too Much?" *Journal of Economic Perspectives* 18(3) (2004), 147–172.

[48] Hans Rosling, with Ola Rosling and Anna Rosling-Rönnlund, *Factfulness: Ten Reasons We're Wrong about the World: And Why Things Are Better Than You Think* (New York: Flatiron Books, 2018).

average temperature of the Earth will rise over the next 100 years. Second, he tells us that most people are pessimistic about poverty, population growth, and vaccination rates. Rosling tells us that although most experts accept that the fraction of people living in extreme poverty was halved between 1995 and 2015, the majority of people do not. However, he also states that even the experts are unaware of the trends underway that predict much lower population growth and much higher rates of vaccination.

I find it interesting that in his book, Ehrlich argued that people did not understand extrapolation bias; he gave dramatic examples to bolster his case that the population was growing too rapidly. In any event, as Rosling notes, the rate of population growth is on a downward trajectory. In respect to climate change, the takeaways from Rosling's work appears to be that most people understand that global warming is underway, are massively ignorant about recent social improvements, and are excessively pessimistic about the state of social conditions in the future.

It strikes me that DICE-2016 embodies the neoclassical view about technology and adaptation emphasized by Simon in the Ehrlich–Simon debate, and the awareness of climate change adjusted for pessimism bias that Rosling emphasized. I would note that the assumptions about population growth Nordhaus makes in DICE-2016 are consistent with the projections Rosling provided.

The differing judgments by mainstream climate scientists and neoclassical economists such as Nordhaus constitute an example of what psychologists refer to as "noise."[49] The message in Section 2 from climate scientists is that the threat from global warming is dire. In contrast, the message in this section is more that the threat from global warming, while important, is not dire.

The stakes associated with these different perspectives are enormous; there-fore, it is vital to understand where the analyses of the two sections agree and where they do not. Moreover, this is not an either/or proposition. Both perspec-tives offer critical insights, and an important piece of behavioral advice is that we need to be careful not to throw out babies with bathwater.

The DICE model plays an important role in this Element, not because it is perfect or complete, but because it can ground a considered discussion about the benefits and costs of global warming policy. There are important lessons to be learned, especially on the behavioral front, by examining both its strengths and its weaknesses. In this respect, DICE provides a coherent structure to push back against and this is what will happen in the remaining sections, which discuss

---

[49] See Daniel Kahneman, Olivier Sibony, and Cass R. Sunstein, *Noise: A Flaw in Human Judgment* (New York: Little, Brown, 2021).

critiques of Nordhaus' analysis. At the same time, keep in mind that the actual emissions trajectory has been closer to behavioral business-as-usual than to Nordhaus' optimal case, let alone the type of trajectory recommended by mainstream climate scientists.

3.11 Key Takeaways

It is important to model how the climate and global economy interact. William Nordhaus received the Nobel Prize in economics for developing an IAM to do just that.

Nordhaus refers to his interactive assessment model by the acronym DICE. The DICE model provides a quantitative characterization of the interaction between climate and global economy. The model seeks to capture how the burning of fossil fuels from global economic activity produces carbon dioxide emissions. In turn, global warming resulting from these emissions has been and will likely continue to cause the Earth's temperature to rise. Rising temperatures will damage the global economy going forward. This damage provides the focal point of what there is to fear.

Nordhaus' DICE model provides a coherent economic framework for analyzing the time value of money. This issue surfaces in consumers' decisions about saving and in firms' capital budgeting processes where cash flows reflect the cost of abatement activity. In line with the neoclassical approach, DICE implicitly assumes that prices will guide people to make individually rational choices in response to their choice environments. The prices in DICE are mostly defined by interest rates that govern saving and investment choices, including choices about emissions abatement.

In a perfectly competitive market that is complete and features no externalities, interest rates can induce saving and investment choices, including choices about emission abatement, which are optimal. However, because intertemporal markets are not complete, there is likely to be market failure with the consequence being nonoptimal choices for investment, abatement, and saving activity. Correcting for market failure requires the use of Pigouvian taxes. The Pigouvian tax associated with carbon dioxide emission is the optimal price of carbon, which reflects its social cost.

One of the most significant features of the trajectory for the social cost of carbon is that it displays a pattern called the carbon-policy ramp. Carbon prices begin low and increase gradually to reflect damages from global warming.

I want to emphasize that the price of carbon is not an end goal. Fundamentally, the critical issue is about how much the global community spends over time to reduce atmospheric carbon concentration. Setting the price of carbon is intended to serve as a signal to induce suitable amounts being invested to address global warming. Along a DICE optimal path, while the economy remains net carbon positive, the trajectory for R&D into low-carbon technologies displays a climate-policy ramp similar to the ramp for the social cost of carbon.

Nordhaus argues that it is possible to use trade policy variables such as tariffs to structure a carbon club in which all countries set the price of carbon equal to the social cost derived from a version of DICE he calls C-DICE. Notably, C-DICE provides insight into the factors that determine the price of carbon in the behavioral business-as-usual case, relative to the social cost of carbon.

The predictions for atmospheric carbon concentration and temperature based upon DICE-2016 are consistent with the scientific perspective described in Section 2. However, the model also predicts that investment in capital, along with technological progress, will cause per capita consumption to increase at a healthy pace during the twenty-first century.

Looked at one way, the DICE long-term projection raises questions about whether the global warming fears described in Section 2 might be exaggerated. Looked at another way, some might ask whether the DICE optimal case is far from describing rational behavior because it misses something extremely important in climate scientists' warnings.

The tension between the prescriptions of mainstream climate scientists and the prescriptions from DICE are a sequel to the twentieth-century debate over population growth between biologist Paul Ehrlich and neoclassical economist Julian Simon. The neoclassical position is that scientists exhibit pessimism bias in respect to people's ability to adapt in response to market forces. Conversely, the position of mainstream climate scientists is that Nordhaus' climate policy recommendations are too little, too late.

4 Behavioral Analysis of the Nordhaus–Stern Debate

In 2006 economist Nicholas Stern provided a perspective on global warming that was closer to that of mainstream climate scientists than the perspective Nordhaus had advanced. Stern was the principal author of a UK government report known as the *Stern Review*. The *Stern Review* recommended trajectories for carbon prices and rates of abatement that were significantly larger than those Nordhaus advised.[50]

In 2007 Yale University hosted a conference to allow Nordhaus and Stern to debate. The debate made clear that the primary difference in modeling

---

[50] Nicholas Stern, *The Economics of Climate Change: The Stern Review* (Cambridge: Cambridge University Press, 2007). https://doi.org/10.1017/CBO9780511817434.

assumptions between the two is the time discount factor, denoted by the symbol ρ. Stern assumed a value of ρ that was much lower than the value Nordhaus assumed. Effectively, Stern suggested that the value of ρ Nordhaus posited was unethical, and Nordhaus contended that Stern's value of ρ was unrealistic.

My view is there are three main takeaways from debate. First, in the context of IAMs, the ethics issue was overblown. Second, the debate failed to address the fact that mainstream climate scientists' concerns were not embodied within the economists' IAMs. Third, both Nordhaus and Stern were unrealistic in respect to actual climate policy. I will offer brief remarks about each of these three points.

On the ethics of abatement: The intuition of many is that the current generation's unwillingness to choose higher levels of abatement will subject future generations to a harsh lifestyle on a much warmer planet. However, this intuition is off. Table 1 makes clear that for both Nordhaus cases, future generations will be much better off than the current generation, even with higher global temperatures. It is difficult to offer a compelling ethical indictment of Nordhaus' optimal case, based on differences in per capita consumption across generations.

On mainstream climate scientists' concerns not being embodied within the economists' IAMs: The *Stern Review* identifies a series of issues that do not appear to play explicit roles in IAMS. The *Review* refers to "severe impacts" resulting from average global temperatures rising "by 2–3°C within the next fifty years" (p. vi). The list of impacts includes more frequent droughts and floods, melting glaciers, declining crop yields, ocean acidification, rising sea levels, weakening of the Atlantic Thermohaline Circulation thereby partially offsetting warming in both Europe and eastern North America, increased mortality due to malnutrition and heat stress, permanent displacement by mid-century of 200 million people, and 15–40 percent of species becoming extinct.

Economist Martin Weitzman suggested that the *Stern Review*'s recommendations might be right for the wrong reason. In this regard, he suggested recasting the analysis into a risk setting in which abatement costs are akin to insurance premiums, with abatement providing a hedge against catastrophic climate damage.[51]

As I discuss in the body of the section, modifying DICE so that global warming damages reflect sufficiently severe impacts gives rise to optimal policies that are consistent with the recommendations in the *Stern Review*. In my view, there is no need to make the case based on a low discount rate and

---

[51] Martin Weitzman, "A Review of the *Stern Review* on the Economics of Climate Change," *Journal of Economic Literature* 45 (September 2007), 703–724.

corresponding ethical argument. Specifically, the ethical argument distracts attention from the issue of damages, which is much more important.

On a related matter, Nordhaus argues that the discount value proposed in the *Stern Review* produces unrealistic features about the trajectories for saving, growth, and return on capital. For Nordhaus, realistic trajectories constitute a behavioral constraint and key trajectories in the *Stern Review* analysis violate that constraint.

On the unrealistic expectations of Nordhaus and Stern: After 2007, trajectories for carbon prices and actual emissions continued to be much closer to behavioral business-as-usual than to the trajectories Nordhaus recommended, let alone those Stern promoted. The reasons economists have had so little influence on actual climate policy are psychological. In Section 5 I focus on the psychological forces that played a large part in the choice of actual climate policy. In this section I focus on psychological elements that neoclassical economists tend to ignore but that exert a major influence on how people make intertemporal choices.

4.1 Nordhaus versus Stern: Setting the Stage

In focusing attention on "severe impacts" resulting from average global temperatures rising by 2–3°C within the next fifty years, the *Review* rejected the contention that mainstream climate scientists exhibited pessimism bias, and implicitly suggested that neoclassical economists such as Nordhaus exhibited optimism bias. Optimism bias involves the attachment of excessively high probabilities to favorable events, and correspondingly excessively low probabilities to unfavorable events.

For his part, Nordhaus noted that the then-current version of DICE yielded an optimal 2015 price of carbon dioxide per ton of $35 (in 2005 dollars US).[52] Moreover, his analysis recommended that the price of carbon increase over time, reaching $85 in 2050 and $206 in 2100. The corresponding optimal rates of emissions abatement are 14 percent for the 2015 period, 25 percent for the 2050 period, and 43 percent for the 2100 period.[53]

Nordhaus (2007) points out that the *Stern Review* estimates the then-current social cost of carbon to be $350 per ton, which is ten times the DICE model counterpart. An article in *The Globe and Mail* described the contrast in policy

---

[52] Nordhaus, "*Stern Review.*"

[53] Nordhaus and Boyer (2000) wrote that the optimal case features a carbon tax that began at $6 per ton for the period 1990 through 1999, and followed a climate ramp pattern in which it increased over time, reaching $13 per ton in 2015, $29 per ton in 2050, and $63 per ton in 2100. See William D. Nordhaus and Joseph Boyer, *Warming the World: Economic Models of Global Warming* (Cambridge, MA: MIT Press, 2000).

recommendations as follows. The *Stern Review* calls for ramping spending on abatement immediately, peaking at 2.75 percent of global GDP by 2012, and then declining to 2.5 percent by 2035. In contrast, Nordhaus recommends a policy ramp beginning at 0.3 percent of global GDP in 2010, reaching 0.6 percent in 2020, and peaking at 0.9 percent in 2065.[54]

The implications of the two policies for atmospheric carbon dioxide concentration and atmospheric temperature are significant. Relative to DICE, for the year 2100, the *Stern Review* recommends having carbon dioxide concentration be less by about 150 ppm, and a global temperature that is lower by approximately 1°C.[55]

4.2 Different Perspectives about Climate Ethics

The *Stern Review* raised important questions about the ethics involving sacrifices related to global warming that early generations make for the benefit of later generations. Ethical judgments are embedded in formal frameworks like those Nordhaus and Stern employed through the utilitarian social welfare function W.[56] Of particular importance is the value of the time discount rate ρ. Nordhaus chose a DICE- annual value of 1.5 percent for ρ, which corresponds to a five-year compounded rate of about 7.7 percent. Recall that DICE uses time periods, or cohorts, having a five-year duration. Therefore, DICE discounts the welfare of a subsequent cohort by 7.7 percent relative to the prior cohort.

The *Review* argues that there is no ethically justifiable reason to favor the prior cohort over its successor, and suggests a rate of near zero instead. Specifically, the *Review* uses an annual rate ρ of 0.01 percent. In this regard, the *Review* takes the position that time discounting at a positive rate constitutes a flaw in human nature.[57]

Nordhaus (2007) states that the main difference between his recommended policy and that of the *Review* stems from the underlying assumptions about the value of ρ, even though the *Review* states that the sharp difference between its recommendations and others stems from the fact that "we treat risk explicitly and incorporate recent evidence on the risks" (p. xvi). Nordhaus points out that

---

[54] See Neil Reynolds, "Pointless to Rush a Carbon Emissions Plan," *The Globe and Mail*, July 2, 2008.

[55] There are excellent analyses of the Nordhaus–Stern debate, one of which is by Frank Ackerman. See Frank Ackerman, "Debating Climate Economics: The *Stern Review* vs. Its Critics Report to Friends of the Earth-UK." Report: Global Development and Environment Institute, Tufts University, Medford MA 02155, USA. www.bu.edu/eci/files/2019/06/SternDebateReport.pdf. However, Ackerman makes no mention of psychology and mentions "behavior" just once, in the context of a puzzling behavior pattern described by economist Martin Weitzman.

[56] See Matthew Rendall, "Discounting, Climate Change, and the Ecological Fallacy," *Ethics* 129 (April 2019), 441–463.

[57] See the appendix to this section for an excerpt from the *Review* on this point.

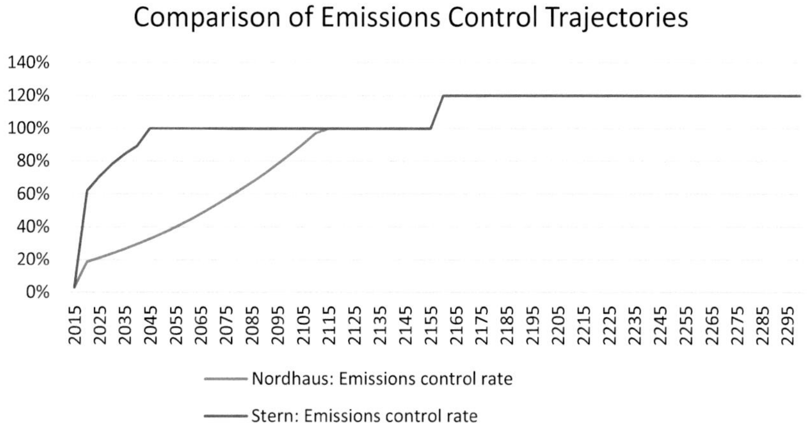

Comparison of Emissions Control Trajectories

Figure 14 Comparison of emission control rate trajectories under Nordhaus' assumptions and assumptions in the *Stern Review*

the analytical structure used in the *Review*, a framework called PAGE, is nearly identical to DICE. This similarity allows Nordhaus to use DICE in order to pinpoint the main factors responsible for the sharp difference in recommendations. To do so, Nordhaus makes two substitutions to the parameter values in his model, replacing the original values with those Stern used. The two parameters are the rate of time discount and the elasticity of intertemporal substitution (EIS = $1/\alpha$). For the first, DICE uses 1.5 percent whereas the *Review* uses 0.01 percent. For the second, at the time of the debate DICE used $\alpha=2.0$ whereas the *Review* uses $\alpha=1.0$.[58] Nordhaus reports that after making these two substitutions, the "2015 optimal carbon price in the DICE model rises from \$35 ... to \$360 per ton."

Figures 14 and 15 contrast the values of the emissions control rate, abatement cost as a fraction of output, and social cost of carbon for the Nordhaus and Stern policies.

Note that in Figure 14 Nordhaus and Stern's trajectories both eventually reach net zero emissions (100 percent abatement). The Stern trajectory does so earlier, in 2045, whereas the Nordhaus trajectory does so in 2115. Thereafter, the two trajectories coincide; when a carbon negative technology emerges in 2160, the two trajectories move to being net carbon negative. (See the discussion in Section 3 regarding Nordhaus' assumption about net negative emissions.)

Figure 14 illustrates a key feature of optimal solutions. They coincide after reaching the point of net zero emissions. Therefore, the critical differences

---

[58] See the appendix to Section 3 for the parameter values Nordhaus chose for DICE-2016. For some parameters, these are different from the values Nordhaus was using in 2007.

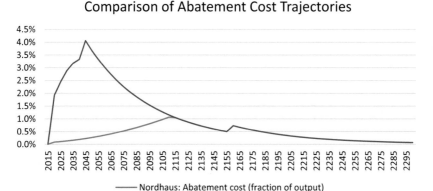

Figure 15 Comparison of abatement cost trajectories under Nordhaus'
assumptions and assumptions in the *Stern Review*

pertain to how quickly the point of net zero is reached and how much abatement
occurs during the lead-up to net zero.

Figure 15 displays the associated abatement cost trajectories. The *Stern
Review* trajectory is much higher during the lead-up to net zero. Figure 16
displays the difference in trajectories for the social cost of carbon.

There is an implicit issue here about idealism versus practicality. Nordhaus
(2007) and other neoclassical economists were quite critical of Stern for
adopting what they regard as an unrealistic rate of time discount. Nordhaus
has consistently argued that an optimal policy must be consistent with historical
rates of return on capital. In this regard, he claimed that a time discount rate of
1.5 percent is indeed consistent, whereas a time discount rate of 0.01 percent is
too low.

My understanding of Stern and Nordhaus' different thinking about climate
change boils down to what constrained optimization means in respect to climate
change. Stern wants us to understand that there is no good reason, a priori, to
penalize people because just because they will be born later in time. Given this
ethical perspective, he wants us to understand what kind of climate policy will
reflect that perspective.[59]

I view Nordhaus as reminding us that pragmatically, we need to craft climate
policy that is appropriate for the world we actually inhabit, not a version of the
world that we wish for but is unattainable. The world we inhabit functions with

---

[59] There is also the problem of grandstanding. Near-infinite altruism toward future generations
does not square with very limited altruism toward poor people today. See chapter 9 of
Riccardo Rebonato, *How to Think about Climate Change: Insights from Economics for the
Perplexed but Open-Minded Citizen* (Cambridge: Cambridge University Press, 2021).

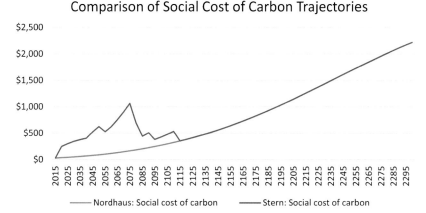

Figure 16 Comparison of social cost of carbon trajectories under Nordhaus' assumptions and assumptions in the *Stern Review*

a global economy that includes capital markets. We are constrained by how capital markets operate and we will not be able to regulate those markets so as to achieve the idealistic outcome associated with the ethical norms espoused by the *Review*. Therefore, we need an optimal policy that corresponds to a constrained optimization with realistic constraints. That is what Nordhaus seeks to do.

For Nordhaus, the issue boils down to interest rates. Time discounting at 1.5 percent a year will bring DICE into alignment with historical rates of return on capital. Nordhaus (1994) used 6 percent as the return on capital, and a slightly lower rate in his later work. Notably, Nordhaus sees no reason to predict that future rates will significantly differ from the past. He contends that time discounting at near zero instead implies interest rates from the model that are too low.[60]

Nordhaus' point is that climate policy has to be right for the interest rate environment that prevails, not an environment that is aspirational but unattainable. This is why he contends that the policy recommendations from the *Stern Review* for carbon pricing and abatement policy are suboptimal for a world with higher interest rates than those in the *Stern Review* analysis.

In Nordhaus' words, "a low real return on capital leads to a very high initial carbon price and very sharp initial emissions reductions. The climate-policy ramp flattens out."

---

[60] Nordhaus uses a "wrinkle in time" thought experiment to argue against the discount rate proposed by Stern. The wrinkle is a tiny damage to aggregate consumption that begins in year 2200 and persists forever. Based on Stern's discount rate, Nordhaus points out people today would be willing to spend an absurdly large amount of money today in order to avoid the wrinkle.

This last remark is important. Recall from Section 3 that the climate-policy ramp is a key feature of Nordhaus' recommended policy. Nordhaus is saying that countries that "front-load" investment in carbon reduction ensure that opportunity costs rise to inappropriate levels. In the language of finance, this means that firms undertake large climate projects with significantly negative NPVs.

How negative? I analyzed how DICE-2016, with Nordhaus' parameters, would evaluate the *Stern Review*'s recommended policy compared to the behavioral business-as-usual case. The behavioral business-as-usual case turns out to be significantly better, despite much higher temperature increases in the former, which eventually approach 7°C, I might add.[61] This point comes up later, in Figure 19 below. In other words, according to DICE-2016, implementing the *Review*'s recommended policy makes matters much worse than doing nothing at all in response to global warming.

For Nordhaus, the institutional setting for making decisions about climate finance is absolutely critical; as a result, it is important to understand exactly how interest rates are formally determined in his model. In Section 3, I discussed this issue from the production side. Nordhaus (2007) explains his use of the classic Ramsey equation for this purpose, which pertains to the demand side. Briefly, the Ramsey equation stipulates that the interest rate is the sum of two terms, the time discount rate and the product of the inverse elasticity of substitution and the growth rate. In the appendix to this section, I discuss the formal issues associated with the Ramsey equation.

4.3 Behavioral Issues in the Spirit of Irving Fisher

The *Review* suggests that we not think of time discounting as being rational. Indeed, many of the sentiments Stern expresses are behavioral in nature, rather than neoclassical. The thing is that being a neoclassical economist, Stern is inclined to use neoclassical models, and neoclassical models have rational behavior at their very foundation. Neither the *Review* nor Nordhaus (1994, 2007) make mention of the work of Irving Fisher, who in 1930 published one of the most important treatises on interest rates, aptly entitled *The Theory of Interest*.[62]

---

[61] Temperature increases in Nordhaus' optimal case are high at 4°C, but nowhere near as high as the 7°C reached in 2025 in the behavioral business-as-usual case.
[62] Irving Fisher, *Theory of Interest: As Determined by Impatience to Spend Income and Opportunity to Invest It* (New York: Macmillan, 1930).

4.3.1 Irving Fisher's Perspective

Fisher was careful about his use of terminology. At one stage, he used the term "time preference" by which he meant time discounting; however, in *The Theory of Interest*, he replaced the term "time preference" with "impatience." He explained that impatience is impacted by at least six factors, which he identified as foresight, self-control, habit, expectation of life, concern for the lives of other persons, and fashion.

Fisher wrote at a time before neoclassical economists became fixated on rationality as a core principle guiding behavior. Fisher certainly qualifies as a behavioral economist, recognizing that some people behave irrationally owing to a lack of foresight or self-control. Notably, he wrote: "As to the irrational aspect of the matter, the effect of poverty is often to relax foresight and self-control and to tempt us to 'trust to luck' for the future, if only the all engrossing need of present necessities can be satisfied" (p. 73).

This last paragraph is especially important for neoclassical economists who are used to thinking of maximizing models as models of rational behavior. Fisher developed a maximizing model to describe behavior; however, he viewed some behavior as irrational. This is an important point, so at the risk of being pedantic, let me reiterate. Fisher regarded imperfect self-control and imperfect foresight as irrational, even if actual choices can be described as the outcome of an optimization.

There are different degrees of irrational behavior. Some irrational behaviors are severe. For example, some people join Alcoholics Anonymous (AA) because they realize they have a severe problem controlling their drinking. Such people drink too much, know they drink too much, and do not think they are making rational choices when they get drunk.

Drinking too much is not just an expression of people rationally valuing the present over the future. Overdrinking is not about rational impatience. For problem drinkers, joining AA might well be a move in the right direction. However, some problem drinkers will procrastinate when it comes to joining AA and such procrastination might be far from being the outcome of rational choice. Irving Fisher recognized this issue, and as I discuss in Section 5, described the drinking problem in an illustrative comment involving a "saloon."

Present bias is a bias for "now" relative to "later." Just to be clear: Valuing the present over the future is not necessarily irrational; however, present bias is about an intense demand for immediacy.

Present bias is about overemphasizing "now" relative to the future. The thing is that now is a moving target. On Monday, now means Monday, and Monday feels much more important than Tuesday, which in turn feels a bit more important than Wednesday. However, a day later, now becomes Tuesday, at which time Tuesday feels much more important relative to Wednesday than it did the day before, on Monday.

Later in the section, I compare two discounting functions for analyzing impatience, one exponential and the other hyperbolic. With exponential discounting the relative weighting of Wednesday to Tuesday stays constant over time, even when "now" shifts from Monday to Tuesday. With hyperbolic discounting the weighting of Wednesday to Tuesday decreases when "now" shifts from Monday to Tuesday. Hyperbolic discounting reflects present bias.

Present bias underlies the "Mañana Effect," meaning procrastinating behavior in which a person always puts off until tomorrow tasks that could be done today. By induction, such tasks never get done before days they have to be done. Some academics might have noticed that their students delay studying until just before tests and exams.

4.3.2 Two-System Thinking and Self-Control

Fisher's ideas about self-control found expression in the work of later economists. My own work with Richard Thaler on the economics of self-control built on several of Fisher's insights.[63] The self-control model Thaler and I developed was the first formal treatment of the two-system approach that Daniel Kahneman (2011) describes as "thinking, fast and slow."[64] Impulse, the expression of being impatient, corresponds to fast thinking, while planning is a slow-thinking activity.

The planner-doer framework featured the first neuroeconomics model, in that it incorporated brain structure into the utility-based approach economists use to study consumer choice. Here the planner is associated with the prefrontal cortex, the locus of executive function activity. The doer is associated with limbic function activity, involving impulses related to needs and wants. Neuroeconomists have identified specific regions of the brain that underlie both and their connection to willpower strength.[65]

In the two-system self-control framework, Thaler and I examined a special case in which "planner" preferences are symmetric in respect to consumption at

---

[63] Richard Thaler and Hersh Shefrin, "An Economic Theory of Self Control," *Journal of Political Economy* 89(2) (1981), 392–406. See also Hersh Shefrin and Richard Thaler, "The Behavioral Life Cycle Hypothesis," *Economic Inquiry* 24 (1988), 609–643.

[64] Daniel Kahneman, *Thinking, Fast and Slow* (New York: Farrar, Straus, and Giroux, 2011).

[65] The specific brain regions are the ventomedial prefrontal cortex (vmPFC) and the dorsolateral prefrontal cortex. The critical issue for willpower involves the relative strength of the latter in respect to the former. See Todd Hare, Colin Camerer, and Antonio Rangel, "Self-Control in Decision-Making Involves Modulation of the vmPFC Valuation System," *Science* 324(5927) (2009), 646–648.

different times. Formally, the planner's preferences exhibit a zero discount rate.[66] However, the act of having to exert willpower in order to restrain fast thinking "doers" typically imposes costs that induce behavior consistent with time discounting. In other words, for this special case, time discounting emerges as a consequence of willpower being costly, not because of underlying ethical values.

"Nudge" is a behavioral term to induce people to change their behavior, for the better, in minimally invasive ways.[67] Fisher suggested that people with limited self-control will save less than what is in their own best interests. The planner-doer framework provides a formal framework to analyze the issue of inadequate savings.

In my work with Thaler, we suggest a series of policies to help people who cannot get themselves to save more. Our suggestions built on our observations of practices people chose for themselves in order to save more. At first glance, these practices appeared to be suboptimal, at least from a neoclassical perspective. For example, some people chose to join Christmas club programs at their savings institutions. These saving programs paid lower interest than other accounts and prohibited withdrawals until the holiday shopping period. Needless to say, in (neoclassical) theory a person could accomplish with a regular account that paid higher interest and had fewer restrictions than a corresponding Christmas club, the same goals for which they use a Christmas club.

The point is that what appears to be rational from a neoclassical perspective might be infeasible psychologically. People do their best, given human nature,

---

[66] We made this assumption to highlight the case of positive discounting reflecting the impact of willpower being a costly activity in respect to mental resources. There is a natural selection-based argument to support time discounting, and for that matter other psychological phenomena such as loss aversion. In a comment on a draft of this manuscript, Riccardo Rebonato states:

> From an evolutionary perspective a preference for the same consumption now rather than later has evolutionary advantages in the real world – as opposed to lab settings – where the "promise" of the same good later may not materialize. I believe that our key preferences – for more rather than less, for more even consumption, for less risk, for sober rather than later – all confer evolutionary advantages, and this is why they developed.

> I concur with this view; however, I would also point out that these advantages apply to different past primitive environments, have been embedded in the system, are not always rational for current, modern environments, and when excessive underlie irrational behavior associated with undersaving and overconsumption of addictive goods such as alcohol, tobacco, and certain types of drugs. I would add that the neuroeconomics literature has identified weak activity in the dorsolateral prefrontal cortex with behavior typically associated with low willpower.

[67] For an excellent critique of the nudge approach, see Riccardo Rebonato, *Taking Liberties: A Critical Examination of Libertarian Paternalism* (London: Palgrave MacMillan, 2012).

but doing one's best when constrained by human nature is not the same thing as being rational in the neoclassical sense.

Subsequently, Thaler and Shlomo Benartzi developed a highly successful savings program they called "Save More Tomorrow" (SMT). Very loosely speaking, SMT is akin to a Christmas club for retirement saving that starts out modestly and increases the saving rate gradually over time, with SMT participants being automatically enrolled but also having the choice to opt out. Building on the success of SMT, Thaler worked with Cass Sunstein to apply the behavioral approach more broadly and called the approach "Nudge."[68]

The DICE social planner is analogous to the individual planner in the planner-doer model. By that analogy, a social planner would not, on ethical grounds, discriminate against people just on the basis of when they appeared in time. To take the analogy one step further, time discounting reflects the cost of willpower, which acts as a constraint on choice.

All of this leads me to suggest that global warming is a self-control problem. In Shefrin (2013) I characterized global warming as a much bigger challenge facing humans than other self-control challenges.[69] Setting the social planner's rate of time discount to be significantly higher than zero does not imply that it is rational to do so. Instead, it reflects the acceptance that humans' capacity for exercising willpower is limited, as are the means at their disposal for dealing with weakness of will.

Just to repeat a point I made in a preceding paragraph: What appears to be rational from a neoclassical perspective might be infeasible psychologically.

In DICE-2016 the global savings rate is approximately 25 percent, which Nordhaus argues is in line with historical data. By way of contrast, the savings rate associated with the *Stern Review* is above 30 percent. Not to put too fine a point on it, but history suggests that 30 percent is idealistic, not realistic.

Of course, what drives the higher *Stern Review* savings rate is the near-zero time discount rate in the *Review*. The point here is that a low-time discount rate impacts all consumption-savings decisions, not just decisions about climate finance.

[68] Richard H. Thaler and Cass R. Sunstein, *Nudge: The Final Edition* (New York: Penguin Books, 2021). See also Richard Thaler and Shlomo Benartzi, "Save More Tomorrow: Using Behavioral Economics to Increase Employee Saving," *Journal of Political Economy* 112(1), pt. 2 (2004) S164–187. Benartzi calls SMT the most successful nudge program in the world, noting that it has helped more than 25 million Americans increase their rate of saving. https://tinyurl.com/2cru3wcd.

[69] See Hersh Shefrin, "Behavioral Economics and Business," in *The Purpose of Business: Contemporary Perspectives from Different Walks of Life*. Edited by Albert Erisman and David Gautschi (New York: Springer [Palgrave-MacMillan], 2013), 193–227.

Very important to understand is that the higher propensity to save in the *Review* analysis, relative to Nordhaus' analysis, implies a lower interest rate in equilibrium. After all, if people are willing to save at a higher rate, they do not need the interest rate to be higher in order to entice them to do so. For example, for the year 2025, "DICE-2016 with Nordhaus parameters" features an interest rate of about 5 percent, whereas "DICE-2016 with Stern parameters" features an interest rate of about 2.5 percent.

The difference between the two interest rates implies that the marginal investment project under Stern's recommended policy has an internal rate of return of 2.5 percent, whereas the hurdle rate in a Nordhaus equilibrium is 5 percent. Therefore, in a Nordhaus equilibrium (be it the behavioral case or the optimal case), the marginal Stern project has a negative NPV. Hence, private sector firms would be unwilling to adopt these projects and it would fall to the public sector to do so, if they had sufficient public support. I would add that this is a big if.

4.3.3 Hyperbolic Discounting and Market Aggregation

Fisher argued that in equilibrium, the market interest rate aggregates varying degrees of impatience across economic agents. In his words, "for society the degrees of impatience of the aggregate of individuals determine, or help to determine, the rate of interest. The rate of interest is equal to the degree of impatience upon which the whole community may *concur in order that the market of loans may be exactly cleared*" (p. 120).

Consider the aggregation issue Fisher describes, as it applies to the Nordhaus–Stern debate. Heal and Millner (2014) provide an analysis of the aggregate time discount rate in a model with several economic agents who differ from each other in respect to time discount rates.[70] Their intent is to find a middle ground between Nordhaus and Stern. Heal and Millner establish that for their model, the market discount rate is time dependent and declines monotonically to the lowest rate in the population. In a standard model, the discount factor is exponential; however, in the Heal–Millner model, the discount factor shares the features of a hyperbolic function. For additional discussion of this point, see the appendix to this section. In respect to ethics, Heal and Millner take the position that ethical intergenerational preferences are subjective, and interpret their aggregation result to imply that the ethics of the market can be represented as an amalgam of the differing ethical values held by economic agents in the population.

---

[70] Geoffrey Heal and Antony Millner, "Agreeing to Disagree on Climate Policy," *PNAS* 111(10) (2014), 3695–3698. www.pnas.org/cgi/doi/10.1073/pnas.1315987111.

4.4 Risk

The *Stern Review* makes two important points. The first, much discussed earlier in this Element, is that actual climate policy at the time, and for that matter the climate policy Nordhaus recommended, do not live up to our higher ethical ideals. The *Review* is very clear to say that zero-time discounting reflects these higher ethical ideals and that positive-time discounting reflects a flaw in human nature.

The second point pertains to risk. The *Review* explains that the sharp difference in its recommended policy from others stems from the fact that "we treat risk explicitly and incorporate recent evidence on the risks." The *Review* states that if the global community fails to act, "the overall costs and risks of climate change will be equivalent to losing at least 5 percent of global GDP each year ... If a wider range of risks and impacts is taken into account, the estimates of damage could rise to 20 percent of GDP or more" (p. vi).

Keep in mind that both Nordhaus and Stern used certainty models to analyze the impact of global warming and of course, certainty models do not incorporate risk. Nevertheless, as I discuss in what follows, they do not ignore risk, but apply Monte Carlo simulation to their models in order to analyze the impact of risk. More recent IAMs incorporate risk explicitly, and I discuss the more recent approach in Section 6.

4.4.1 Trajectories for Carbon Dioxide Concentration and Atmospheric Temperature

With risk in mind, consider what DICE-2016 implies about the trajectories for atmospheric temperature and carbon concentration, first under Nordhaus' assumptions and then under the *Review's* assumptions. Figures 17 and 18 display the comparisons.

The most striking feature of the comparison displayed in Figure 17 is that under the *Stern Review* trajectory, carbon concentration peaks in year 2045 at 433, while under Nordhaus' assumptions, carbon concentration peaks much later, in year 2110 at 639.

The implications for atmospheric temperature are sharp. Under the *Stern Review* assumptions, atmospheric temperature peaks in year 2140, at 2.5°C, whereas under Nordhaus' assumptions, atmospheric temperature peaks in about the same year, but at 4°C. See Figure 18 in this regard.

4.4.2 Climate Risks

One way to think about Figures 17 and 18 is to ask why, from a risk perspective, the *Stern Review* temperature trajectory is superior to the Nordhaus temperature

Atmospheric Carbon Dioxide Concentration

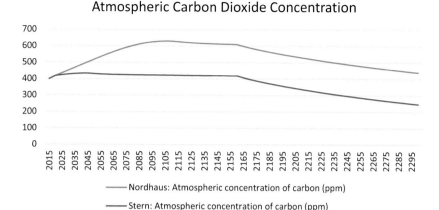

———— Nordhaus: Atmospheric concentration of carbon (ppm)

———— Stern: Atmospheric concentration of carbon (ppm)

Figure 17 Comparison of atmospheric carbon dioxide concentration trajectories, using DICE-2016, under Nordhaus' assumptions and assumptions in the *Stern Review*

Atmospheric Temperature Above Preindustrial

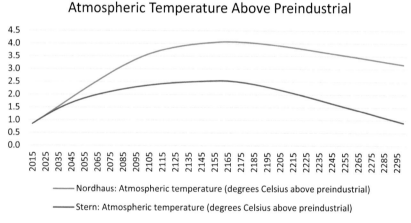

———— Nordhaus: Atmospheric temperature (degrees Celsius above preindustrial)

———— Stern: Atmospheric temperature (degrees Celsius above preindustrial)

Figure 18 Comparison of trajectories for atmospheric temperature above preindustrial, using DICE 2016, under Nordhaus' assumptions and assumptions in the Stern Review.

trajectory. My sense from the language in the *Review* is that, time discounting aside, Stern attaches more weight to the damage associated with higher temperatures than does Nordhaus. The language, which I mention elsewhere in this section, includes passages such as the following: "[T]he social cost of carbon today, if we remain on a BAU trajectory, is of the order of $85 per tonne of CO_2 – higher than typical numbers in the literature, largely because we treat risk explicitly and incorporate recent evidence on the risks" (p. xvi). Here BAU is an acronym for business-as-usual. The *Review* also emphasizes risks related to loss of species, human deaths from shortages of food and water, and irreversible changes to the Earth's system. Additional detail appears in the appendix to this section.

In a thoughtful essay about the policy recommendations in the *Review* Weitzman (2007) suggested the following: "The basic issue here is that spending money to slow global warming should perhaps not be conceptualized primarily as being about consumption smoothing as much as being about how much insurance to buy to offset the small change of a ruinous catastrophe that is difficult to compensate by ordinary savings."[71] Weitzman stated that the *Review* might be right in its recommended policy, but for reasons associated with catastrophic risk, not the discount rate.

Consider Weitzman's point about catastrophic risk, in conjunction with Nordhaus' point about IAM assumptions needing to produce realistic values for the return on capital. Nordhaus tells us that the *Stern Review* parameter values produce a savings rate that is unrealistically high and in consequence a return on capital that is unrealistically low. Hence he rejects the *Stern Review* parameter values in favor of his own.

I accept Nordhaus' point, which amounts to a behavioral constraint, meaning a constraint on how people actually behave, in this case reflecting the degree of impatience. People might intellectually accept a low discount rate on ethical or other grounds, but psychologically, people do not always behave in accordance with what they accept intellectually. Specifically, when it comes to the rate at which people save, they might well behave in accordance with a higher discount rate than they accept intellectually. Analogously, problem drinkers might want to abstain from alcohol but have difficulty resisting the temptation to have a drink.

The last point is important for making assessments of policy using an IAM such as DICE. The utilitarian objective function in DICE depends on both the savings and the carbon price trajectories. If the savings trajectory is biased, so will be the value of the DICE-objective function. A higher savings rate will typically lead to a larger capital stock, higher future production, and higher future emissions. The assumption of higher saving rates than the values produced by DICE-2016 is akin to the establishment of a global successful SMT-nudge program. As noted earlier, SMT has achieved considerable success, albeit far from global success.

To reiterate: If the optimal saving rate trajectory based on the *Stern Review* parameter values cannot be trusted, then the associated optimal carbon price trajectory and emissions trajectory likewise cannot be trusted. With the behavioral constraint on rate of return to capital in mind, consider Weitzman's point. Consider what kind of damage risks would lead to the *Stern Review*

---

[71] Weitzman, "Review of the *Stern Review*."

recommendations about social cost of carbon and abatement, but with Nordhaus' parameter values.

Among the list of risks the *Review* identifies, I would focus on the tipping point issue.[72] For example, one tipping point relates to methane, a GHG that is about 28 times as potent as carbon dioxide and that has contributed 20–30 percent of anthropogenic global warming. A large volume of methane resides in permafrost. If the permafrost melts, large pools of methane will begin to enter the atmosphere, further warming the planet and causing the release of yet more methane.

Consider a modification to the damage function in DICE-2016 so that it includes tipping point events with significant consequences.[73] Given Nordhaus' choice of parameter values, but for the modified damage function, the optimal emissions control trajectory is very similar to trajectory associated with the *Stern Review*. The same statement applies to the social cost of carbon. In respect to Nordhaus' behavioral constraint, the interest rate and saving rate trajectories associated with the modified damage function are close to those in Nordhaus' original optimal solution.

In summary, the inclusion in DICE of plausible assumptions about tipping points leads to an abatement trajectory similar to that in the *Stern Review*, but that passes Nordhaus' behavioral constraint involving the return on capital. I view this as support for Weitzman's position that the ruinous catastrophe climate risk is by far a larger issue than the discount rate. Moreover, the optimal emissions trajectory in the modified model is chosen to prevent any tipping point from occurring because the future consequences are so severe.[74]

4.4.3 Thoughts on the Fundamental Tension

The *Stern Review*'s discussion of risk is in line with the warnings of mainstream climate scientists, which brings us back to the tension between mainstream climate scientists and neoclassical economists such as Nordhaus. As discussed in Section 3, the issue here is akin to the Ehrlich–Simon debate: how adept will humans be at adapting to the increase in global temperature?

Consider the optimistic perspective, where the risks are small and the realized trajectories are fairly close to those projected by DICE-2016. In this situation, think about the nature of the intergenerational conflict in the Nordhaus optimum.

---

[72] For a discussion of tipping points in the IPCC reports, see www.ipcc.ch/sr15/chapter/chapter-3.

[73] In the modification tipping points occur at every 0.5°C increase, beginning at 1.5°C. Between 1.5°C and 3.5°C damages successively rise at respective tipping point temperatures by factors of 2, 4, 6, 8, and 10. While the modification is weaker than what some climate scientists suggest, it is sufficiently strong to support the abatement trajectory recommended in the *Stern Review*.

[74] Put differently, the point here is that it is the threat of tipping point damages, not a low discount rate, which induces a higher social cost of carbon and corresponding lower emissions than in the original DICE-2016 counterparts.

In Section 3 I mentioned that, in DICE-2016, the cohort in year 2100 will experience per capita consumption of approximately $52,000, whereas the cohort in year 2015 will experience consumption of approximately $15,000. Remember that the $52,000 is net of abatement costs and damage from global warming.

The difference between the optimal case and the behavioral business-as-usual case for the 2100-cohort is about $170. In the context of DICE-2016, we are asking whether it is ethically desirable for the 2015-cohort to sacrifice some of its $15,000 consumption, which is approximately 29 percent of what the 2100-cohort will consume, in order to improve the living standards of the 2100-cohort by $170 per person.

Not to put too fine a point on it, but $170 constitutes 0.03 percent of an increase relative to the behavioral business-as-usual case – not a lot. Of course, it is not just the 2100-cohort that would benefit from the sacrifice made by the 2015-cohort, but all subsequent cohorts, most of whom are expected to have a higher standard of living than the 2015-cohort.

With this last paragraph in mind, consider what changing the time discount rate from 1.5 percent to 0.1 percent will do to the ethical case for asking the 2015-cohort to make the sacrifice.[75] In the context of DICE-2016, a lower time discount rate will lead the optimal solution to call for even more sacrifice from the 2015-cohort in order to widen the disparity between its living standard and the living standards of subsequent cohorts. In this case, the zero discount rate case features the $170 being replaced by $1,500.

The trade-off discussed in the preceding paragraphs is hardly what mainstream climate scientists are concerned about. Climate scientists are worried, among other things, about the current generation making sacrifices to prevent future generations from experiencing standards of living much worse than their own. Their concern is not with justifying increases in per capital consumption of the order $170 or $1,500 for future generations who they expect will experience standards of living more than three times greater than their own.

4.4.4 Did Nordhaus Ignore Risk?

In their respective formal analyses both the *Stern Review* and Nordhaus' analyses take risk into account. Despite suggestions in the *Review* to the contrary, Nordhaus' analysis did not ignore risk.

---

[75] Keep extrapolation bias in mind here: compounding over the course of 50 or 100 years will greatly amplify what might seem like a small difference in annual discount rates. Using a discount rate of 1.5 percent implies that relative to the current generation, the welfare of a generation 100 years hence is 22.5 percent, whereas for a discount rate of 0.01 percent it is 99 percent.

For its IAM, the *Stern Review* uses a framework called PAGE, which stands for Policy Analysis of Greenhouse Effect. Overall, PAGE is similar in structure to DICE and its regional counterpart RICE (Regional Dynamic Integrated model of Climate and the Economy).[76] It is structured to perform risk analysis using Monte Carlo simulation. At the same time, DICE is also so structured: see the section entitled "Monte Carlo Estimates" in chapter 6 of Nordhaus (1994). In describing revisions to the DICE/RICE framework, Nordhaus and Boyer (1999) state: "The new models separate the impacts into catastrophic and non-catastrophic components, but the overall economic impacts of climate change for the next century or so are little changed from earlier DICE/RICE analyses."[77]

Notably, PAGE partitions the world into eight geopolitical regions. In addition, PAGE focuses on a whole range of GHGs, including carbon dioxide, which it divides into six main classes. The *Stern Review* will often measure atmospheric concentration of all GHGs in carbon dioxide equivalents, for example stating: "The risks of the worst impacts of climate change can be substantially reduced if GHG levels in the atmosphere can be stabilised between 450 and 550ppm CO_2 equivalent (CO_2e)" (p. vii).

I would add that RICE partitions the world in thirteen regions. Early versions of RICE focused on all GHG emissions, but later versions shifted the focus to industrial carbon dioxide emissions.

All of this suggests that Nordhaus' formal analysis of risk was not dramatically different from the analysis in the *Review*. That said, there is an important point to make about biased judgments of tipping point risk in Nordhaus' analysis. Nordhaus and Sztorc (2013) write about DICE-2013:

> The current version assumes that damages are a quadratic function of temperature change and does not include sharp thresholds or tipping points, but this is consistent with the survey by Lenton et al. (2008).
>
> Figure 2 shows the results of the Tol (2009) survey on damages, the IPCC assessment from the Third and Fourth Assessment Reports, and the assumption in the DICE-2013 R model as a function of global mean temperature increase (p. 11).

In the foregoing passage, the Lenton in Lenton et al. (2008) is Tim Lenton, a climate scientist from the University of Exeter.[78] He serves as the director of the Global

---

[76] Dmitry Yumashev, "PAGE – ICE Integrated Assessment Models," Working Paper, Pentland Centre for Sustainability in Business, Lancaster University, 2020. See www.researchgate.net/publication/342396462. See also William D. Nordhaus, with Joseph Boyer, "Roll the DICE Again: The Economics of Global Warming," Working Paper, Yale University, 1999.

[77] Nordhaus and Boyer, "Roll the DICE Again."

[78] Timothy M. Lenton, Hermann Held, Elmar Kriegler et al., "Tipping Elements in the Earth's Climate System," *Proceedings of the National Academy of Sciences* 105 (2008), 1786–1793; William D. Nordhaus, *The Climate Casino* (New Haven, CT: Yale University Press, 2013);

Systems Institute and as chair in Climate Change and Earth System Science. In recent work Lenton takes exception to this passage and contends that the exclusion of tipping points in DICE is actually inconsistent with the contents of his survey.[79] This critique suggests serious bias in the DICE assumptions about damages from global warming and raises questions about confirmation bias on Nordhaus' part in respect to information that does not confirm his views about such damages.

The second paragraph in the last quoted passage refers to work by Richard Tol about damage estimates. Nordhaus eventually acknowledged the downward bias in Tol's estimates.[80] For additional discussion on what Nordhaus stated about Tol's estimates, see the appendix to this section.

I remind readers that regardless of issue relating to Tol's estimates, the damage function in DICE-2016 is still quadratic in temperature increase and does not embody tipping points. Figure 19 displays how the difference in temperature projections differs between DICE-2013 and DICE-2016. The upward revision for both the behavioral business-as-usual case and the optimal case is a clear indication of excessive optimism bias.

While Nordhaus has come under criticism for under weighting the left tail of the outcome distribution, he has criticized others for under weighting the right tail. In covering the aftermath of the Nordhaus–Stern debate, the media reported Nordhaus' view that trillions of dollars of assets might be stranded by a single technological advance that could occur in the middle of the current century.[81]

4.5 The Debate's Indiscernible Impact on Actual Climate Policy

Consider that the Nordhaus–Stern debate had no discernable impact on actual climate policy, as trajectories for emissions and carbon prices continued to be business-as-usual. According to DICE-2016, with Nordhaus' parameter values, the social cost of carbon (dioxide) in 2020 was about $37 per ton, and will increase to $44 in 2025 and $51 in 2030. According to the *Stern Review*, using DICE-2016 with Stern's parameter values, the social cost of carbon was about $250 per ton in 2020, and it will increase to $300 in 2025 and $344 in 2030.

Here is a stark reality: Nordhaus' and Stern's estimates differ not just from each other, but also from the actual global average price of carbon, which in

Timothy M. Lenton and Juan-Carlos Ciscar, "Integrating Tipping Points into Climate Impact Assessments," *Climatic Change* 117 (2013), 585–597.
[79] Steve Keen, Timothy M. Lenton, Antoine Godin et al., "Economists' Erroneous Estimates of Damages from Climate Change," submitted to *The Royal Society*, 2021.
[80] Nordhaus, "Revisiting the Social Cost of Carbon."
[81] Reynolds, "Pointless to Rush a Carbon Emissions Plan."

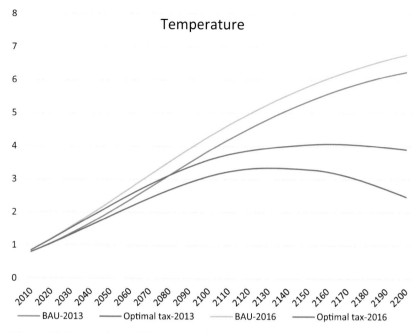

Figure 19 Comparison of four atmospheric temperature projections, relating to DICE-2013 and DICE-2016, for behavioral business-as-usual cases and optimal cases. The vertical axis is in °C above preindustrial times.

2021 the International Monetary Fund (IMF) estimates to have been about $3 per ton.[82]

The IMF analysis indicates that only 20 percent of carbon dioxide emissions are priced. Moreover, the current average price of $3 is far less than the $75 price that the IMF maintains is needed to keep the atmospheric temperature increase below 2°C, the global target negotiated in 2015 as part of the Paris climate agreement.[83]

Not put too fine a point on it, but the $3 IMF estimate is actually much closer to the carbon prices in the behavioral business-as-usual case, which are $2.21 in 2020 and increasing to $2.44 in 2025 and to $2.69 in 2030. In other words, the behavioral business-as-usual case comes much closer to reflecting the real-world

---

[82] Ian Parry, "Five Things to Know about Carbon Pricing," International Monetary Fund, *Finance and Development*, September 2021.

[83] In 2022 the IMF recommended an international lower bound carbon price policy, with different countries in different categories being subject to different floor levels. The categories are: $25 for low-income countries, $50 for middle-income countries, and $75 for high-income countries. See Jean Chateau, Florence Jaumotte, and Gregor Schwerhoff, "Why Countries Must Cooperate on Carbon Prices," International Monetary Fund, May 19, 2022. https://bit.ly/3YG5TVY.

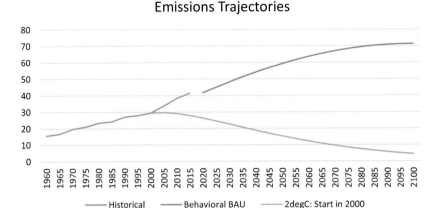

Figure 20 Comparison of trajectories for global emissions of carbon dioxide. Units are Gt. Sources: Historical data are from Our World in Data. Behavioral BAU are from DICE-2016. 2degC: Start in 2000 is from Our World in Data, Robbie Andrews, based on data from the Global Carbon Project.

pricing of carbon dioxide than either the Nordhaus optimal case or its *Stern Review* counterpart.

Consider what this last point looks like graphically. Figure 20 displays three trajectories for global atmospheric carbon dioxide emissions for the period 1960 through 2100. The left-most trajectory is historical. The middle trajectory portrays carbon dioxide emissions that would be compatible with the global atmospheric temperature remaining below 2°C. The third trajectory corresponds to the behavioral business-as-usual case.

The middle trajectory portrays a plausible outcome had the global community found a way to exhibit sufficient self-control in response to Nordhaus' urging back in 1997. However, it did not, as can be seen from the historical trajectory after the year 2000 and, as I suggested earlier, the current trajectory is closest to behavioral business-as-usual.

Figure 21 adds three series to Figure 20. The first is a trajectory similar to the middle trajectory, but beginning in 2010, shortly after the Nordhaus–Stern debate. The second and third additions are the trajectories associated with Nordhaus and the *Stern Review*, based on DICE-2016.

Notice in Figure 21 that the *Stern Review* trajectory is the most aggressive, with emissions abatement being much sharper than what it would have been had appropriate abatement begun in 2000. The additional aggressiveness is largely a consequence of needing to ramp up more quickly because of procrastination.

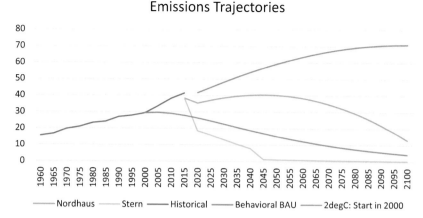

Figure 21 Comparison of trajectories for global emissions of carbon dioxide. Units are Gt. Sources: Historical data are from Our World in Data. Behavioral BAU, Nordhaus, and Stern are from DICE-2016. 2degC: Start in 2000 is from Our World in Data, Robbie Andrews, based on data from the Global Carbon Project.

In contrast, the Nordhaus trajectory is less aggressive than the trajectory associated with abatement beginning in 2000. This is largely because Nordhaus' optimal case does not limit temperature increases during the twenty-first century to being below 2°C, but instead to being below 3.5°C.

There is something important to understand about tipping points and the Weitzman critique. Suppose that a tipping point damage function replaces the Nordhaus quadratic function in DICE-2016, with the optimal abatement policy being something like the policy recommended by the *Stern Review*. In this case, the reduced emissions will be sufficient to avert a climate tipping point catastrophe. However, if the abatement policy chosen conforms to behavioral business-as-usual, the climate will experience a tipping point and corresponding catastrophe.

The Nordhaus and *Stern Review* trajectories displayed in Figure 21 begin in 2015, almost a decade after the Nordhaus–Stern debate. Following the debate, the positions of Nordhaus and Stern remained far apart for quite some time.

After Nordhaus received the 2018 Nobel Prize in economics the Grantham Institute at the London School of Economics, headed by Stern, reviewed Nordhaus' accomplishments and positions.[84] The title of a commentary from

---

[84] Bob Ward, "A Nobel Prize for the Creator of an Economic Model That Underestimates the Risks of Climate Change," Grantham Institute Commentary on January 2, 2019. https://bit.ly/3sn69Nu.

the Institute was: "A Nobel Prize for the Creator of an Economic Model That Underestimates the Risks of Climate Change."

In a 2020 presentation Stern made clear that the concerns mainstream climate scientists had expressed were at the top of his mind.[85] He focused on these issues much more than the pricing of carbon. Indeed, in his presentation, he made no mention of a specific carbon price, but did criticize IAMs for underestimating the impact of tipping points.

Over time, the positions of Nordhaus and Stern moved toward each other. Stern's prescription for a global carbon price, for 2017, declined to about \$100.[86] In 2021, Nordhaus' prescription of a global carbon price increased to about \$100.[87] In respect to the failure of the United States to institute a national carbon price, Nordhaus characterized the failure as being on an "island of fiscal denial" and reiterated his position that a carbon tax was essential to efficiently reaching the nation's climate goals.

In 2022, forty-three years after the release of the Charney report, the United States passed global warming legislation as part of the Infrastructure Investment and Jobs Act ((IIJA) and the Inflation Reduction Act (IRA). The IRA authorizes approximately 0.15 percent per year of US gross domestic product (GDP) to be spent on a variety of abatement activities.[88] For the time period in question, a decade, this percentage is in line with Nordhaus' DICE-2106 optimal expenditure on abatement, but far less than the 2–3 percent called for by the *Stern Review*. To benchmark these figures, let me say that in 2017 the United States spent 0.21 percent of its GDP on new investment in new power and fuels. In that year global investment in new power and fuels was 0.34 percent of world GDP, with China's contribution to total investment in alternatives having been 45 percent, and that of the United States having been 15 percent.[89]

Notably, the US legislation did not include a provision for a national carbon tax. After the bill was passed and awaiting signature by President Biden,

---

[85] Nicholas Stern, "The Economics of Sustainable Growth in an Uncertain World: Urgency, Scale, Choice," Presentation from Grantham Institute, London School of Economics, 2020. Stern lists his affiliations as IG Patel Professor of Economics & Government, London School of Economics and Political Science; Chair of the ESRC Centre for Climate Change Economics and Policy; Chair of the Grantham Research Institute on Climate Change and the Environment; Co-chair of the Global Commission on the Economy and Climate (New Climate Economy).

[86] Nicholas Stern and Joseph Stiglitz, "Getting the Social Cost of Carbon Right," *Project Syndicate*, February 15, 2021. https://bit.ly/3P3c3MT.

[87] "Nobel Winner's Evolution from 'Dark Realist' to Just Plain Realist on Climate Change," *Washington Post*, June 14, 2021. https://bit.ly/3sjzBUP.

[88] The IRA was crafted in such a way that there is no cap on spending. See https://bit.ly/47FuRc2.

[89] *Renewables 2021: Global Status Report*. https://bit.ly/3shz8lW. See also *Renewables 2018: Global Status Report*. Global new investment was \$280 billion in 2017 and rose to \$303.5 billion in 2020.

Nordhaus described the legislation as the first step along a journey, which if it also proved to be the last step would result in "a fiery future."[90]

I should note that, in DICE, the social cost of carbon need not be a tax. Nor need it be the price in a cap-and-trade system. Rather it is anything that induces an increase in the current rate of abatement, such as a subsidy that induces higher current costs but lower future damages.[91] At the time, based on models discussed in the appendix to Section 6, the Environmental Protection Agency (EPA) estimated the social cost of carbon to be approximately $190 per ton. Notably, the EPA's estimate was more in line with the perspective of the *Stern Review* than with that of Nordhaus.[92]

In respect to Figure 21, there is reason to hope that with the passage of the climate legislation in the United States, there will be a movement from the behavioral business-as-usual trajectory in the direction of the Nordhaus trajectory. As discussed in Sections 1 and 2, the United States is only part of the global economy and no longer the largest emitter of GHGs.

In recent years, researchers have worked to modify the DICE IAM in at least three important ways. For a discussion about these modifications, see the appendix to this section.

4.6 Key Takeaways

The Nordhaus–Stern debate was a watershed event for clarifying important issues about the economic modeling of climate change. I suggest that the main differences between Nordhaus and Stern are behavioral in nature, reflecting both limited self-control and judgmental biases.

The debate clarified that Nordhaus' optimal case refers to efficiency in the sense of identifying the broad outline of a cost-benefit–based, realistic global response to the threat posed by global warming. This optimal case features a gradual climate-policy ramp, in respect to both the social cost of carbon and abatement activity. Under Nordhaus' optimal policy, the point of net zero emissions is reached in year 2115. In contrast, for Nordhaus' behavioral business-as-usual case, the point of net zero emissions does not arrive until year 2240, when the global temperature will have increased by almost 7°C relative to preindustrial times.

---

[90] Coral Davenport and Lisa Friedman, "Five Decades in the Making: Why It Took Congress So Long to Act on Climate: The Senate Bill Avoided the Political Pitfalls of Past Legislative Attempts by Offering Only Incentives to Cut Climate Pollution, not Taxes," *New York Times*, August 7, 2022. www.nytimes.com/2022/08/07/climate/senate-climate-law.html.

[91] See the appendix to Section 3, which discusses a series of issues pertaining to competitive equilibrium, including subsidies and taxes.

[92] See https://bit.ly/47EQLwo.

The *Stern Review* argued that Nordhaus' optimal case relies on a rate of time discount that is not ethically defensible. This is because DICE heavily discounts the welfare of future generations relative to earlier generations. The *Review's* optimal case-based recommendations call for an abrupt increase in the social cost of carbon and magnitude of abatement activity, with the point of net zero emissions arriving in year 2045.

Nordhaus argued that ethical values are not unique. Indeed, in his framework a Rawlsian social planner would favor earlier generations over later generations, not the reverse. Nordhaus also emphasized that the *Stern Review* recommendations cannot be implemented by a global private sector with well-functioning capital markets. This is because the recommendations from the *Review* feature unrealistically high savings rates and unrealistically low interest rates. In a setting with realistic interest rates, the *Review*'s recommendations would require the selection of projects with very negative NPVs.

There are important questions that received very little attention in the debate, especially when comparing alternative climate policies. Two of these are: When does a policy recommend reaching the point of net zero emissions? When does a policy recommend reaching the point of net negative emissions?

The *Review* reiterated the concerns of mainstream climate scientists about the risk of future major damages that will result from global warming if such warming is uncontained. Weitzman clarified that the *Review's* recommendations might be appropriate when viewed as an insurance premium to hedge against catastrophic risk.

The economics literature clarified that Nordhaus' assumptions about future damage from global warming are biased downward, in line with excessive optimism. In particular, Nordhaus' damage function does not feature tipping points and the associated catastrophic risk.

Appropriately modifying Nordhaus' damage function to incorporate tipping points can lead to an optimal policy that is similar to the one recommended in the *Review*, but with realistic rates for saving and interest. This is in line with Weitzman's position.

For his part, Nordhaus suggests that his critics' position exhibits excessive pessimism about future technological progress that would lead to rapid decarbonization at relatively low cost. Excessive optimism and excessive pessimism are both behavioral phenomena. Both Nordhaus and Stern appear confident in their positions and both cannot be right. At least one is overconfident.

Irving Fisher emphasized that time discounting reflects impatience arising from a lack of both foresight and self-control. Along with the aforementioned biases, these are important behavioral issues. Plausibly, anthropogenic global warming represents the most significant collective self-control issue in human history.[93] In the next section I discuss how the global community has fared thus far in facing its self-control challenge, how it has dealt with vulnerability to bias, and what lessons it has learned or ignored from the Nordhaus–Stern debate.

Although the Nordhaus–Stern debate generated important insights, there are three issues to keep in mind. First, in the context of IAMs, the ethics issue was overblown. Second, the debate failed to address the fact that mainstream climate scientists' concerns about the negative impacts of anthropogenic global warming, especially tipping point phenomena, were not embodied within the economists' IAMs. Third, Nordhaus and Stern's expectations were unrealistic in respect to actual climate policy.

5 Psychology, Politics, and Climate Policy: Unsettling Behaviors

Psychology and politics have been the primary drivers of climate policy, not recommendations by economists based on IAMs. As I continue to mention, actual policies have been more in line with business-as-usual behaviors than with the recommendations made by most mainstream climate scientists and economists. Why psychology and politics have combined to produce these unsettling behaviors is what I call the "big behavioral question." The big behavioral question is the subject of this section, the focus of which is the psychological dimension of climate politics as it developed in the United Stated from 1980 on.

In my view, the global community's reluctance to veer from business-as-usual behaviors is tantamount to aggregate procrastination and trusting to luck. Procrastination results from weak self-control, leading to "present bias." Trusting to luck reflects aspiration-based risk seeking and the aversion to accepting a sure loss.

Some neoclassical economists might believe that the answer to the big behavioral question is new, improved IAMs. In my view, this belief is misguided. There is no evidence to suggest that the global community ignored the recommendations made by economists because of flawed IAMs. However, there is strong evidence that neoclassical economists stripped away the psychological components of models developed by their classical economist predecessors and new improved IAMS, which I will discuss in Section 6, continue to omit these components.

---

[93] Some might argue that because damages from current emissions will mostly impact future generations, self-control is not germane. My view is that this view holds only if there is no bequest motive. As I point out in the appendix to Section 3, the IAM literature lacks clarity in identifying how the social planner optimal case would be achieved as part of a decentralized competitive equilibrium, in which households/consumers make utility-maximizing decisions about saving, firms make value-maximizing decisions about capital accumulation, and government policymakers make optimal decisions about the price of carbon. In particular, I emphasize the importance of treating household preferences as reflecting the utilities of future generations, so as to align individual household preferences and social planner preferences.

Irving Fisher emphasized lack of foresight and self-control as major determinants of the irrational impatience preventing people from saving more than they do. Fisher tells the story of a farmer who would not mend his leaky roof because when it was raining, he was unable to stop all the water from leaking in. When it was not raining, there was no leaking water with which to be concerned.

The analogy is too close for comfort. In Section 2 I discussed the congressional testimony of Carl Sagan from 1985. Sagan articulately made the strong point that if the global community acted quickly, the threat from global warming could be contained at low cost; however, he warned that the costs from delayed action would be much higher. In the analogy 1985 corresponds to "it is not raining."

Continuing with the leaky roof–global warming analogy, today it is raining. Perhaps it is not yet raining hard, but it is raining nonetheless, enough to create discomfort. In the summers of 2022 and 2023, record heat waves were occurring in the southern part of the United States, Southern Europe, the UK, and China. The media headlines made clear the discomfort,[94] which gave rise to articles describing worse outcomes that are expected to come.[95] Notably, the heat waves have caused droughts that have depleted water flows that normally generate hydroelectric power. Hydroelectric power is a major source of clean electricity, the reduction of which raises the pressure to increase reliance on fossil fuels such as coal.

Irving Fisher was clear to distinguish between lack of self-control and lack of foresight. He recognized that while their effects might be similar, the causal mechanisms differed. In this regard, he wrote that while foresight pertains to thinking, self-control pertains to willing. As an example of weak will, he described those "workingmen" who are unable to resist the temptation of the "saloon" while making their way home. For him such behavior represented the inability to deny oneself "a present indulgence," even in the knowledge of

---

[94] Jon Henley, "Europe's Rivers Run Dry As Scientists Warn Drought Could Be Worst in 500 Years:

  Crops, Power Plants, Barge Traffic, Industry and Fish Populations Devastated by Parched Waterways," *The Guardian*, August 13, 2022. https://bit.ly/3OJIkXV. See also Sha Hua and Yang Jie, "China's Scorching Heat Leads to Power Cuts, Factory Disruptions: Foxconn, VW, Toyota Plants Hit in Sichuan: Crop Output Also Affected China's Yangtze River Dries Up As Heat Wave Disrupts Factories." *Wall Street Journal*, August 17, 2022. https://bit.ly/45DHKlr; Daniel Trotta, "Explainer: What's Causing the Recent US Heat Waves?" Reuters, August 17, 2022. https://bit.ly/45e83id.

[95] John Muyskens, Andrew Ba Tran, Anna Phillips, Simon Ducroquet, and Naema Ahmed, "More Dangerous Heat Waves Are on the Way: See the Impact by Zip Code. By Mid-century, Nearly Two-Thirds of Americans Will Experience Perilous Heat Waves, with Some Regions in the South Expected to Endure More Than 70 Consecutive Days over 100 Degrees." *Washington Post*, August 15, 2022. https://bit.ly/47wVaBr.

the "consequences" to follow.[96] Today we understand that it is typically dopamine flows associated with present indulgences that give rise to potential self-control difficulties.[97]

I suggest that the reluctance to institute an appropriate global carbon price is analogous to Fisher's working men being reluctant to forego visiting a saloon. The issue is lack of willpower, not lack of foresight, as the "consequences" are clear. In the case of global warming, ever since the release of the Charney report mainstream climate scientists have stated very clearly what the consequences would be from continued emissions of GHGs into the atmosphere.

For his part, Nordhaus has been promoting the idea of a global price for carbon since the 1980s.[98] His climate-policy ramp recommendation shares important features with the nudge program Save More Tomorrow, SMT, mentioned in Section 4, which was designed to help people overcome self-control challenges to increase saving. In 1997 Nordhaus was quoted in the *New York Times* as urging the United States to institute a carbon pricing policy. He said at the time: "Let's do something modest, but let's really do it."[99]

To date, no such policy has been instituted on a global basis, although individual countries such as Canada have done so. Notably, Nordhaus' gradual climate-policy ramp shares some of the nudge components in SMT. Indeed, Thaler and Sunstein, the authors of *Nudge*, suggest calling the climate-policy ramp "Green More Tomorrow." To the extent that carbon taxes, once instituted, become difficult to phase out, the climate-policy ramp becomes the default, subject to the inertia associated with status quo bias.

Saving rates and carbon prices are the two control variables in DICE. Both saving rates and carbon prices feature the potential for nonoptimal choices stemming from psychological pitfalls. In the United States the contrast between SMT and Green More Tomorrow is striking. Save More Tomorrow has been widely adopted and highly successful at helping Americans save more. Green More Tomorrow, or at least its climate-policy ramp structure, has not been adopted.

Psychological pitfalls are at the heart of the big behavioral question, meaning the global community's procrastination in dealing sensibly with the threat posed

---

[96] Fisher, *Theory of Interest*, 83.
[97] Anna Lembke, *Dopamine Nation: Finding Balance in the Age of Indulgence* (New York: Dutton, 2021).
[98] See William Nordhaus and Gary Yohe, "Future Carbon Dioxide Emissions from Fossil Fuels," in *Changing Climate: Report of the Carbon Dioxide Assessment Committee* (Washington, DC: National Research Council, 1983). In 1991 Nordhaus published a paper that offered the first cost-benefit analysis of abatement policy. See William D. Nordhaus, "To Slow or Not to Slow: The Economics of the Greenhouse Effect," *Economic Journal* 101(407) (1991), 920–937.
[99] Peter Passell, "Until Payoff Is Clear, Haste Means Big Waste," *New York Times*, December 1, 1997.

by anthropogenic global warming. At the core is a failure of self-control: impatience, the absence of sufficient willpower, and the inability to defer immediate gratification.

The planner-doer model of self-control-based present bias treats the individual as if it were a collective composed of different agents, each with its own preferences. In the present section I describe how the individual-based perspective and the collective-based perspective both contribute to the strong presence of present bias in climate policy.

The psychology underlying climate politics is complex and involves a series of additional phenomena.[100] In the remainder of this section I discuss the role these phenomena have historically played in humans' response to the global warming threat.

Section 5 makes little reference to economic analysis. There is a lot to say about psychology and politics. Because much of the content in the section lies outside the sphere of issues economists typically focus upon, there are reasons to be concerned about availability bias. Psychological issues in particular do not come readily to neoclassical economists' minds. The section's length reflects my attempt to counter this manifestation of availability bias.

5.1 The Psychology of Risk

The psychology of risk is a framework for understanding the cognitive and emotional elements that underlie how people manage risk. By cognitive elements I refer to issues such as the framing of outcomes in terms of gains and losses relative to reference points, as well as heuristics and biases associated with judgments about risks being faced. By emotional elements I refer to issues such as fear, hope, and the aspirational need to feel successful.[101]

Nathaniel Rich (2018) documents the response during the 1980s to the release of the Charney report in 1979. His research provides detail about memos, meetings, and personalities.[102] He contends that during the 1980s, the global community seriously began to consider the warnings about climate change and yet the end result was business-as-usual. Rich makes an important point about fear, asking whether the level of collective fear was sufficient to induce the enactment of cost-benefit–based climate policy.

Fear is one of the major elements in the psychological approach to risk that was developed by psychologist Lola Lopes. She called her framework SP/A theory,

---

[100] These include the psychology of risk, status quo bias, groupthink, regret and responsibility, aversion to ambiguity, cognitive dissonance, motivated reasoning, limited attention, and trust.

[101] Psychologists Daniel Kahneman and Amos Tversky focused on cognitive issues while psychologist Lola Lopes focused on emotional issues.

[102] Rich, "Losing Earth."

where S represents security, P represents potential, and A represents aspiration.[103] In what follows I describe the general features of SP/A theory and discuss how to embed SP/A theory in the two-system planner-doer model of self-control.

In SP/A theory the emotions of fear and hope operate by distorting perceptions of probability. Fear operates on probability beliefs by increasing the probabilities attached to unfavorable outcomes, relative to other outcomes. Hope operates on probability beliefs by increasing probabilities attached to favorable outcomes, relative to other outcomes. In this respect, being fearful is similar to being pessimistic while being hopeful is similar to being optimistic. Lopes points out that it is possible to be "cautiously hopeful," whereby the probabilities of both highly unfavorable and highly favorable events are over weighted relative to the probabilities attached to middle-range outcomes.[104]

The A in SP/A theory reflects aspiration and is modeled as the probability of meeting or exceeding a specified aspirational level, called a "focal point." The level of the aspirational level reflects the degree of ambition. The importance of meeting or exceeding the focal point is modeled as the relative strength of the A variable relative to the combined effects of fear and hope.

In SP/A theory people make choices among risky alternatives in order to address their needs of fear, hope, and the successful achievement of aspirations. They seek security to help alleviate feelings of fear. They seek potential in order to actualize their feelings of hope. They seek risks that offer them the opportunity to achieve their aspirations. According to SP/A theory, the relative strength of these three emotions are the key determinants of how they choose among risky alternatives.

A key feature of the psychology of risk is that people's willingness to take risk depends on both their personal traits and the circumstances in which they find themselves. The same person can be risk averse in some circumstances and risk seeking in others. For example, some people set very high aspirations and attach great importance to achieving an outcome that meets or beats those aspirations. These people tend to be willing to take risks that feature low expected payoffs but offer a relatively high probability of meeting or beating their aspiration levels. However, in the absence of opportunities that allow them to meet their aspirations, they may act conservatively in respect to how much risk they bear.

---

[103] Lola Lopes, "Between Hope and Fear: The Psychology of Risk," *Advances in Experimental Social Psychology* 20 (1987), 255–295. See also Lola Lopes and Greg Oden, "The Role of Aspiration Level in Risky Choice: A Comparison of Cumulative Prospect Theory and SP/A Theory," *Journal of Mathematical Psychology* 43(2) (1999), 286–313. https://doi.org/10.1006/jmps.1999.1259.

[104] Technically fear and hope are associated with change of measure functions. Fear is represented as a concave function of cumulative probabilities while hope is represented as a convex function of cumulative probabilities. Cautious hope is represented by a convex combination of a concave and convex function and has the shape of an inverse S.

Self-control entails the executive portion of a person's brain being able to exercise control over his or her emotional impulses. In the planner-doer two-system framework, the emotions associated with fear, hope, and aspiration are experienced contemporaneously with the impulse for current consumption.[105]

Current emotions and impulses are modeled as being situated with the doer or system 1. The relative strength of these stimuli governs the expression of willpower in respect to the person's decisions regarding current consumption, current saving, and risk exposure in respect to investing wealth. The planner, or system 2, operates on these stimuli in order to impact the behavior of the entity. However, planner activity is costly in terms of mental resources.

In the planner-doer framework the combination of low mental resources and a weak neural technology can lead to a large gap between the planner's preferred behavior and the full person's actual behavior. This gap can take the form of imprudent risk taking because people's emotions lead them to take risks against their better judgment. This is what Irving Fisher meant when he wrote that limited self-control leads people to trust to luck. Psychologically, trusting to luck entails aspiration-based risk seeking, especially in the domain of losses.

5.2 1993: An Unsettling Dark Nudging Campaign to Prevent the Imposition of a Carbon Tax

In 1993 there was a serious attempt in the United States to institute a carbon tax, but the attempt failed. During the prior period of 1979–1992 there was much discussion but little action in the US response to the warnings issued by most mainstream climate scientists. Although President Jimmy Carter supported a major initiative to invest in alternative energy, his successor Ronald Reagan did not. Reagan instead set high aspirations for economic growth, which predisposed him to pursue a policy that featured more climate risk. George H. W. Bush succeeded Reagan as president. While Bush was more disposed to being proactive about global warming than Reagan, Bush's chief of staff was not, the result of which was climate inaction. For additional detail on the period 1979–1993, see the appendix to this section.

Pricing carbon at its social cost is one of the fundamental recommendations by mainstream economists. Indeed, a primary objective of the integrated assessment approach is to estimate a cost-benefit–based trajectory for carbon prices. Therefore, the failure in 1993 to pass a carbon tax was monumental.

---

[105] See Hersh Shefrin, "Unfinished Business: A Multicommodity Intertemporal Planner–Doer Framework," *Review of Behavioral Finance* 12(1) (2020), 35–68. https://doi.org/10.1108/RBF-10-2019-0148. This paper describes the structure of general planner-doer model featuring impulses from multiple sources, as well as risk and uncertainty.

At the time the carbon tax was described as "a BTU tax."[106] The main opposition to passage of the BTU tax came from fossil fuel interests, whose concern related to stranded asset risk, meaning the risk that fossil fuel assets would lose most of their value as alternative energy sources replaced fossil fuels.

Koch Industries, the largest privately held firm in the United States, played a key role in the political efforts to prevent passage of carbon tax legislation. Koch Industries was led by two brothers, Charles and David Koch. Notably, the Koch brothers had funded the Cato Institute, a libertarian think tank. The Cato Institute warned that once passed, a carbon tax would be almost impossible to remove. Members of the fossil fuel industry took this warning to heart. Intuitively, they understood the importance of status quo bias in respect to the establishment of initial (default) positions.

At the time, the Democratic Party controlled both the House of Representatives and the Senate. Clinton and Gore pressured House members to vote for the BTU tax and the Senate then took up the issue.

The Koch brothers also funded a group called Citizens for a Sound Economy, which mobilized political activity at the grassroots level. Charles Koch communicated his concern about the BTU tax to this group, after which the group contacted the American Petroleum Institute to develop a political strategy to fight passage of the BTU tax provision of the Clinton budget. What came out of their collaboration was a two-part plan.

The two-part plan focused on an Oklahoma senator named David Boren, who chaired the Senate Finance Committee. Energy production is an important part of Oklahoma's economy. In the first part of the plan the industry ran an ad in Oklahoma warning that the BTU tax would be very costly to Oklahoma's consumers. In the second part of the plan, members of Citizens for a Sound Economy participated in a campaign to bombard Senator Boren with messages about the ad, expressing great concern about the BTU tax.

Elected officials prefer to be reelected. Senator Boren interpreted the communications he received as a groundswell of spontaneous opposition that threatened his political position. He did not see it an orchestrated political tactic. Boren announced that because he was concerned that the BTU tax would harm American consumers, he would withdraw support for it. President Clinton needed Boren's support to pass the budget and, as a result, the president withdrew the carbon tax provision from his budget proposal.

The tactics used to defeat the BTU tax qualify as dark nudging, meaning nudging that serves the interests of the nudger, but not necessarily the nudgee. The dark nudgers successfully employed three specific elements of the nudge

---

[106] BTU stands for British Thermal Units.

approach, namely Boren's incentives, the choice architecture Boren employed in dealing with the president's proposed budget, and Boren's misunderstanding of how actions mapped onto consequences.[107] In respect to the third element, the misunderstanding involved representativeness bias, as Boren employed stereotypic thinking to interpret the anti-tax messages he was receiving, and availability bias, which is the tendency to rely on information that is readily available and salient.

The psychological dimension of global warming politics is significant and has the two-system approach at its core. In the case of Citizens for a Sound Economy, dark nudging focused on members' fast thinking system 1, which relies heavily on emotional elements, not facts. Facts are inputs to slow-thinking system 2, not the intuitive processes in system 1.

Keep in mind that system 1 involves heuristic stimulus-response functions that analyze current stimuli using patterns stored in their memories. These patterns are tagged with emotional information, known as somatic markers, measuring degree of affect (goodness or badness).[108] Fast thinking is automatic and feels effortless relative to deliberative slow thinking. The "affect heuristic" is a term for making quick decisions by relying on emotional information. Affect-based heuristics tend to be habitual in nature and therefore constitute the default, with system 2 effort required to override the behavior prescribed by system 1.

Overall, much of the American public's system 1 was programmed to associate negative feelings to the BTU tax; conceivably, those impacted lacked the foresight and the self-control to counter that programming. In 1994, which featured midterm elections, Republicans campaigned on the promise to reduce taxes. The campaign turned out successfully for them and for the first time since 1952 Republicans took control of both houses of Congress.[109] House Democrats felt that their support for the BTU tax had hurt them at the polls.

In 1993 the message to Oklahomans in advertisements sponsored by the fossil fuel industry was that passage of the BTU tax would mean that almost every activity they undertook would be taxed, from filling their automobile tanks with gasoline to taking a shower. These messages create somatic markers that associate negative affect to the losses associated with a carbon tax, without any links to its benefits. These are messages earmarked for system 1 thinking, and at that time, any link to benefits from combating climate change would have

---

[107] The leaders of Citizens for a Sound Economy certainly understood Boren's interests, both in respect to the policy value of BTU tax and in being reelected.

[108] See Antonio R. Damasio, *Descartes' Error: Emotion, Reason, and the Human Brain* (New York: Avon, 1994). Also see Paul Slovic, Melissa L. Finucane, Ellen Peters, and Donald G. MacGregor, "The Affect Heuristic," *European Journal of Operational Research* 177 (2007), 1333–1352.

[109] Davenport and Friedman, "Five Decades in the Making."

to come from stodgy, effortful slow thinking system 2. In other words, the United States had and continues to have a serious self-control problem when it comes to pricing carbon at its social cost.

Somatic marker capital is entrenched; it is part of human capital, wired into peoples' brains. Looking ahead, this explains why in 2022 Senator Ron Wyden was forced to accept that a carbon tax was viewed only as a "stick" and that the approach needed to be framed as a "carrot" in the form of subsidies to invest in new abatement technologies. This was a move in the right direction; however, the failure to price carbon dioxide emissions near any reasonable estimate of the social cost of carbon means that it does not go far enough.

The 1980s and 1990s were a period when humans, to use Irving Fisher's paradigm, had a leaky roof over their head but did not have to contend with rain. The 2020s have arrived, it has begun to rain, and the leak is noticeably bigger. Mainstream economists almost universally endorse the need for carbon dioxide to be priced globally at its social cost yet policy hardly reflects recommendations from IAMs. Instead, GHG emissions still evolve along a behavioral business-as-usual trajectory.

5.3 2010: The Unsettling Failure to Enact Cap-and-Trade Legislation

In 2010 President Barack Obama sought to pass a cap-and-trade bill that would limit carbon dioxide emissions and thereby induce a higher price on carbon dioxide. As had happened with the BTU tax, the Koch brothers used the group Americans for Prosperity, which they funded, to undertake a grassroots campaign aiming to defeat the proposal. As had happened with the BTU tax, the House of Representatives passed the cap-and-trade bill; however, the grassroots effort successfully focused on key senators.[110] As had happened twelve years before, the outcome of the subsequent midterm elections resulted in the Democrats losing control of both houses of Congress.

As had happened in the previous decade, opponents of climate action continued to broadcast messages aimed at recipients' somatic markers, associating climate policy with costs but no benefits. For example, Grover Norquist is a political agent who is well known for his efforts to minimize taxes. His organization does so by supporting Republican candidates who sign a pledge not to support tax increases and opposing Republican candidates who do not. Similar to the 1993 campaign in Oklahoma, which associated only "losses" to

---

[110] The election of Barack Obama produced an energetic political backlash against Obama's legislative priorities, especially national healthcare. There was great resistance from the libertarian-leaning segment to the Affordable Care Act, which came to be called Obamacare. Working through Americans for Prosperity, the Koch brother added the opposition to climate change public policies to their anti-regulation agenda.

a carbon tax, Norquist's messaging emphasized that a carbon tax is a tax on almost every consumer activity from driving automobiles to heating homes to flying to vacation spots. Clearly Norquist appealed to people's vulnerability to experiencing present bias.

In 2010 the Koch brothers' strategy for blocking cap-and-trade legislation was much larger and more sophisticated than the bootstrap strategy that in 1993 had blocked passage of a carbon tax. Of profound importance was the momentum the effort by Americans for Prosperity generated. With the Koch brothers' guidance, grassroots groups worked to make climate change a litmus test for which Republican candidates would receive grassroots support and which not. This strategy echoed the Grover Norquist approach to taxes.

The evidence is clear that the Koch brothers successfully reshaped the political position of the Republican Party about collective action to fight global warming. The contrast between registered Democrats and registered Republicans on this issue is stark. In 2021, almost 70 percent of registered voters supported a carbon tax in which all tax revenues are distributed to consumers. In 2021 Democratic support was much stronger than Republican support, with degree of support being 92 percent of liberal Democrats and 82 percent of moderate/conservative Democrats. The counterpart figures for Republicans are 63 percent of liberal/moderate Republicans and 32 percent of conservative Republicans.[111]

Messages to conservative Republicans about associating negative affect to climate policy were especially effective. In a 1992 paper psychologists Dale Griffin and Amos Tversky contended that people are much more persuaded by the strength of arguments than the weight of evidence.[112] Evidence consists of facts, the weight of which is processed by slow-thinking system 2. In contrast, what generally makes arguments effective is the strength of their impact on fast-thinking system 1.

System 1 activity plays an important role in confirmation bias. For those seeking to influence others' system 1, there is a first impression effect. Once a mental construct is tagged by affect, confirmation bias sets in, and people do not easily change their impressions. Nevertheless, they can change, if they encounter a strong enough stimulus. Frank Luntz, who I mentioned in Section 2, changed from being a climate skeptic to being an abatement activist. Why? He was forced to evacuate his Los Angeles home during the Skirball Fire in 2017, an event seared in his memory.

---

[111] *Politics & Global Warming*, September 2021. Yale Program on Climate Change Communication, George Mason Center for Climate Change Communication.

[112] Dale Griffin and Amos Tversky, "The Weighing of Evidence and the Determinants of Confidence," *Cognitive Psychology*, 24(3) (1992), 411–435.

5.4 After 2010: Unsettling Polarized Politics

The success of the Koch brothers' initiative effectively ensured that after 2010, Republicans would resist all congressional efforts to pass meaningful legislation about addressing global warming. The initiative was so successful that the United States has no carbon tax.

The success of this initiative occurred in the face of 70 percent of Americans having indicated support for a revenue-neutral carbon tax. It occurred despite groups such as the Climate Leadership Council (CLC) bringing together moderates consisting of both Republicans and Democrats to advocate for a revenue-neutral carbon tax. These moderates consisted of prominent figures such as George Shultz, James Baker, Hank Paulsen, Larry Summers, and Janet Yellen. It occurred despite significant organized political activity from Citizens' Climate Lobby, which rallied grassroots support for a very specific revenue-neutral carbon tax proposal.

The revenue-neutral carbon tax is similar to the carbon tax dividend policy used in Canada. There is an important framing issue with this policy. As I discuss in the appendix to Section 4, within the DICE framework, in the end it is consumers who pay the carbon tax.

Almost thirty years after the failed effort to institute a BTU tax, the United States passed the IIJA and the IRA, which contained the first significant set of climate provisions. However, these provisions excluded a carbon tax. This was not for lack of effort by elected officials such as Senator Ron Wyden, who chaired the Senate Finance Committee and made every effort to include a carbon tax among the IRA's provisions.

A major source of opposition came from Progressive Democrats, who were concerned that a carbon tax would severely impact low-income households. Progressive Democrats gave little weight to the fact that Canada had instituted a carbon tax in which they rebated the tax proceeds directly to Canadian households. The policy adopted by Canada is referred to as a "carbon dividend" or a revenue-neutral tax. I think the reluctance by Progressive Democrats to support a carbon tax constitutes a case of confirmation bias on the part of Progressives, or perhaps their voting base.

Senator Wyden made every effort to overcome the opposition from Progressive Democrats by excluding gasoline from any proposed carbon tax. High gasoline prices are a major concern for low-income households. In any event, in the end, opposition from one particular senator, Joe Manchin from the energy-producing state of West Virginia, was the decisive factor. Manchin held the pivotal vote.

5.5 Unsettling Psychological Issues Involving ESG Investing

Environment, social values, and governance (ESG) investing focuses on issues related to the environment, social values, and governance. The Koch family foundation would shift its attention to resisting ESG initiatives.

Environment, social values, and governance investing had a predecessor, namely socially responsible investing.[113] For decades a minority of investors have focused on nonfinancial aspects of their portfolio holdings, as well as on financial returns.[114] These investors want their investments to generate positive social impact as well as financial returns. In consequence, some investors hold stocks of firms they regard as socially responsible and shun stocks of firms they regard as socially irresponsible.

Over time, but especially after 2010, the focus on social responsibility was extended to become a focus on ESG. Around 2020 interest in ESG grew dramatically and became a major investment concept.

The psychological issues associated with ESG are important, as ESG is a term that is vague as well as broad. Different investors interpret the concept differently, and it is difficult to measure. Therefore, different metrics give rise to different assessments. As a result, investors are vulnerable to greenwashing because the quality of ESG is in large part subjective and experienced emotionally through system 1.

A subset of ESG investing is called impact investing. Think of impact investors as having more specific ESG goals than other ESG investors. Recent research documents that many impact investors define impact using the sustainable development goals (SDGs) established by the United Nations.[115] There are seventeen such goals. In respect to the "E" in ESG, SDG number 7 is "Affordable and Clean Energy" while goal number 13 is "Climate Action."

Some impact investors are highly focused on SDGs 7 and 13. Relative to all seventeen SDGs, funds invested in goals 7 and 13 lie in the upper-middle range. At the same time, there is evidence that impact investors associate goal 7, but not the closely related goal 13, with relatively high financial returns.[116] This

---

[113] Philipp Krueger, Zacharias Sautner, and Laura T. Starks, "The Importance of Climate Risk for Institutional Investors," *Review of Financial Studies* 33(3) (2020), 1067–1111. See also Laura T. Starks, "Environmental, Social, and Governance Issues and the *Financial Analysts Journal*," *Financial Analysts Journal* 77(4) (2021), 5–21.

[114] Meir Statman, "What Investors Really Want," *Financial Analysts Journal* 66(2) (2010), 8–10.

[115] Timo Busch, Falko Paetzold, and Sarah Louise Carroux, "Unlocking the Black Box of Private Impact Investors," *Qualitative Research in Financial Markets* 14(1) (2022), 149–168.

[116] Falko Paetzold, Timo Busch, Sebastian Utz, and Anne Kellers, "Between Impact and Returns: Private Investors and the Sustainable Development Goals," *Business Strategy and the Environment* 31(7) (2022), 3182–3197.

might be because renewable energy projects are perceived as being profitable than other climate mitigation efforts.[117]

Impact investors need to be concerned that their efforts to shift portfolio weights from brown firms to green firms might backfire. Such a shift might well increase the cost of capital for brown firms. Certainly emissions from brown firms are much greater than from green firms. However, all firms, but especially brown firms, increase emissions when their costs of financing increase; therefore, the efforts of well-intentioned impact investors might increase rather than reduce total emissions.[118]

After 2020 the financial services industry and regulatory agencies greatly increased their focus on ESG investing.[119] Large financial institutions, such as BlackRock, the largest private investment firm in the world, sought to use their proxy power to induce private sector behavior to be less myopic about the long-run impact of their emissions. While clearly in the spirit of ESG as an expression of ethics, BlackRock subsequently clarified its messages. The clarified messages stated that given the increased importance investors are attaching to ESG, good ESG behavior by firms will be reflected in high financial returns, and vice versa.[120]

In the United States, states with large fossil fuel interests structured a coordinated political response to BlackRock and ESG investors through state treasurers. The response entailed the threat of not engaging the services of financial services firms that engage in ESG.[121] The Koch family foundation provided financial support to treasurers in key states, urging them to divest state

---

[117] This finding is important for ocean-based CDR and methane removal GGR. Firms such as Seafields are profit-centered, producing and selling useful products. But not so methane removal, which, at least for now, does not generate revenues from useful products.

[118] See Samuel Hartzmark and Kelly Shue, "Counterproductive Impact Investing: The Impact Elasticity of Brown and Green Firms," Working Paper, Boston College and Yale School of Management, 2023.

[119] See Ye Cai and Seoyoung Kim, 2022. "ESG Greenwashing and the Recent SEC Actions," *Journal of Investment Management* 20(4), 1–3.

[120] Relatedly, Engine No. 1, activist shareholders of ExxonMobil, forced a change in the firm's board in order to increase the firm's profitability. See Christopher M. Matthews, "Exxon vs. Activists: Battle over Future of Oil and Gas Reaches Showdown: Shareholders Vote Wednesday on a Bid for Four Board Seats by Investors Seeking a Company Commitment to Reach Carbon Neutrality by 2050," *New York Times*, May 25, 2021. https://bit.ly/3YIZERy. ExxonMobil had been generating inferior returns by overinvesting in fossil fuel projects. It had also funded campaigns seeking to move emission trajectories away from behavioral business as usual. In addition, it had been funding carbon capture projects, but only to use the carbon dioxide to facilitate more fossil fuel extraction. Hartzmark and Shue (2023) suggest that activist investors, rather than impact investors, are far more likely to induce a reduction in total emissions.

[121] See Matthew Goldstein and Maureen Farrell, "BlackRock's Pitch for Socially Conscious Investing Antagonizes All Sides," *New York Times*, December 23, 2022. https://bit.ly/44dM6yw.

holdings in financial firms such as BlackRock, CitiBank, Bank of America, and J. P. Morgan.[122]

Part of the regulations pertaining to ESG involves firms being required to account for their emissions, both direct and indirect, with associated disclosures. Direct exposures, referred to as Scope 1 and 2, pertain to emissions involving the firm itself: here Scope 2 refers to emissions stemming from the firm's use of electricity, while Scope 1 refers to emissions stemming from non-electricity sources. Scope 3 refers to emissions associated with the firm's supply chains.

In a way, the regulatory framework can be regarded as a substitute for pricing carbon directly. Nordhaus has suggested, and I concur, that pricing carbon at its social cost would induce the desired emission behaviors at much lower cost than relying on regulation. This view, is of course, consistent with the behavioral theme of the section.

5.6 Psychology of Unsettling Behaviors Stemming from Skepticism and Denial

In February 2015 it snowed in Washington, DC. That event led Senator James Inhofe of Oklahoma to bring a large snowball onto the floor of the US Senate as an indication that the globe was not warming.

The Republican Party line had shifted to denying that climate change was a real phenomenon. "Climate denial" became Republican doctrine. In making the shift, the Republican Party reinforced the message of climate change skeptics who for almost three decades had been challenging the validity of the arguments and conclusions from mainstream climate scientists. In 2017 President Donald Trump, a Republican, publicly called anthropogenic global warming a "hoax," withdrew the United States from the Paris climate agreement, and appointed climate skeptics to a variety of positions in his administration.

The activities of climate change skeptics were well documented in the book *Merchants of Doubt* by Naomi Oreskes and Erik Conway (2010).[123] Psychologically, the creation of doubt exploits the combination of cognitive dissonance, aversion to ambiguity, and trust.

Dissonance arises from simultaneously holding conflicting views and resolving it requires that one view be chosen over the other. Typically, the basis for the choice depends on which view is more comfortable. In this regard, anthropogenic climate change being harmful is certainly less comfortable than it being harmless.

[122] See Wesley Muller, "Louisiana Conservatives Consider Ban on Liberal Business Agendas," *Louisiana Illuminator*, December 23, 2022. https://bit.ly/3QL8koy.
[123] Naomi Oreskes and Erik M. Conway, *Merchants of Doubt: How a Handful of Scientists Obscured the Truth on Issues from Tobacco Smoke to Climate Change* (New York: Bloomsbury Press, 2010).

Aversion to ambiguity refers to the discomfort attached to facing uncertainty. Messages about climate science being unsettled emphasize ambiguity and uncertainty.

Most people do not form their views about science by reading scientific documents. Instead they rely on information and messages provided by others, especially from others they trust.[124] Psychological studies indicate that four aspects underlie how much trust people place in a source. The first is the degree to which the source is a "friend" rather than a "foe." The second is the degree to which the source is viewed as exhibiting "ethical integrity." The third is the perceived competence of the source. The fourth is the degree to which the source is predictable or consistent over time.

The merchants of doubt were masters at using uncertainty to introduce dissonance and portraying themselves as worthy of trust. In the appendix to this section I discuss the psychological issues that were pertinent to some of the main skeptics.

5.7 Unsettling Psychological Issues in Global Political Dynamics

The United Nations established the United Nations Framework Convention on Climate Change (UNFCCC), which provided the framework for annual conferences to address global warming. These conferences were called COP, an acronym for Conference of the Parties, which were numbered sequentially beginning in 1995.

During the 1990s the most important COP was COP3, which in 1997 took place in Kyoto, Japan. A major goal of COP3 was the establishment of a global agreement to reduce carbon dioxide emissions below 1990 levels. Vice President Al Gore played a key leadership role at COP3. Despite his efforts, the US Congress refused to ratify the Kyoto Protocol. A key reason for this reluctance is that it called for the United States to limit emissions much more than developing countries. Keep in mind that at that stage, the United States was the world's largest contributor to GHG emissions.

Nordhaus' carbon club theory emphasizes using carbon prices to structure international climate agreements for addressing the free-rider problem. The Kyoto process failed to produce a stable grand coalition to address global warming. Nordhaus identifies free riding as the main obstacle and argues that the absence of sanctions was a critical mistake that doomed the process from the outset.[125]

---

[124] Marianna Pogosyan, "Who Do You Trust? The Psychology of Trust and How to Build It across Cultures,"*Between Cultures*, June 5, 2017. https://bit.ly/3QQhGzn.

[125] Nordhaus amplifies his remarks to say the following:

In October 1997 President Bill Clinton convened an international conference in Washington, DC, in an effort to promote a coordinated global policy for addressing global warming that would involve developing nations. At the conference Clinton emphasized that the US Congress would not support a carbon tax, but suggested instead that the global community focus on two initiatives. The first was a market for trading emissions credits and the second was investment in high-technology alternative energy sources.

Nordhaus participated at this conference and offered a set of critical remarks. He stated that the administration's proposals understated the "size and complexity of the undertaking." He also asserted that it would not be possible "to introduce these wondrous technologies unless we increase the cost of energy."[126] In effect, Nordhaus suggested that these proposals reflected excessive optimism and over-confidence on the part of the administration. Nordhaus' remarks had little effect as psychology and politics, not economics, drove climate policy. The failure to enact a BTU tax in the 1990s and the unwillingness of the US Congress to support the Kyoto Protocol made it difficult for the United States to play an active leadership role on the global stage; this pattern continued into the twenty-first century.

Three subsequent COP meetings stand out. COP15 took place in Copenhagen in 2009. There was great anticipation that this COP would lead the global community to come together around a meaningful climate policy. However, just before the meeting, a cyber hacking event took place at the University of Anglia, involving emails of some of the major climate scientists who were studying global warming.

The hackers searched through a large volume of emails to cherry-pick phrases suggesting that climate scientists were manipulating data to support their recommendations. For example, the hackers focused on scientists' use of the word "trick" to give the impression that climate scientists were attempting to trick or deceive the public about the validity of anthropogenic global warming. As any physicist or mathematician knows, in context the word "trick" means a clever analytical technique, not a deception. Even physicists who qualify as

---

The result of free-riding is the failure of the only significant international climate treaty, the Kyoto Protocol, and the difficulties of forging effective follow up regimes ... Conceptually, the Kyoto Protocol was a climate club with no sanctions ... [T]he Kyoto Protocol was doomed from the start. It did not contain sufficient economic glue to hold a cooperative coalition together ... One difficulty with the use of differentiated emissions targets in the Kyoto Protocol was its stab-in-the-back instability. The initial allocation of permits across countries is a zero-sum distribution. It can generate the same instability as the example of the negotiation over the division of the surplus. One of the attractive features of a regime that focuses on carbon prices is that it can operate as a single-dimensional choice and thereby avoid stab-in-the-back instability.

[126] Greenwire, "Climate Change: Prez Says Developing Nations Must Commit," October 7, 1997.

climate change skeptics should know this. If they had sufficient integrity they would stand up publicly and correct the record. I suggest that the last statement especially applies to atmospheric physicists who are emeritus professors from prestigious American universities.

The COP15 hacking event, which came to be called "climategate," successfully derailed the momentum that had built up prior to the meeting in Copenhagen. No meaningful agreement emerged from the meeting as the focus of climate scientists shifted to responding to the smear. Needless to say, there was no progress at COP15 on instituting a mechanism to price carbon dioxide at its social cost.

Keep in mind Nordhaus' recommendation that the price of carbon be used as the defining inclusion/exclusion criteria for carbon club membership. In March 2009 James Hansen warned about the need for any climate agreement to include a carbon tax. He reminded the global community that during the prior two years, the situation had deteriorated much more quickly than had been anticipated; he said flat out that the required abatement activity could not occur without an appropriate carbon tax.

The world had to wait until COP21 for a climate agreement, which took place in 2015 in Paris. As I said, keep in mind Nordhaus' strong recommendation that the price of carbon be used as the defining inclusion/exclusion criteria for carbon club membership. Keep in mind what Nordhaus told us about why the Kyoto Protocol failed, namely the absence of real sanctions to incentivize parties to the agreement.

John Kerry, who was the secretary of state in the Obama administration, led the US delegation to Paris. Kerry and Hansen met before the meeting. Hansen urged Kerry to push for a global carbon price. Kerry resisted, insisting that pledges were sufficient.

I suggest that Kerry was not just excessively optimistic in his judgment, but overconfident (about his ability). Just after the Paris agreement was concluded, with no global carbon price, I wrote in *Forbes* that the agreement was akin to a New Year's resolution that is unlikely to be kept.[127] Not to put too fine a point on it, but most people lack the self-control required to keep their New Year's resolutions.

Christiana Figueres served as the executive secretary of the UNFCCC when the Paris agreement was negotiated. Figueres was very clear to say that it would have been politically impossible to incorporate carbon pricing into the agreement, referring to the concept as "economists' perfection."[128]

---

[127] https://bit.ly/3QLI8uN.

[128] David Leonhardt, "The Problem with Putting a Price on the End of the World: Economists Have Workable Policy Ideas for Addressing Climate Change. But What if They're Politically Impossible?" *New York Times*, April 9, 2019. https://bit.ly/3shK9ng.

Perfection might mean the optimal solution to a model, but the real world is another matter. In my view, the key issue is not perfection but procrastination. Committing to a carbon price means committing to making sacrifices in the present. It is present bias that stands in the way of pricing carbon sensibly, not striving for perfection. It is Irving Fisher's concept of "trusting to luck," hoping to beat the odds that the nations of the world will live up to the agreement they signed in Paris. It is aversion to accepting a sure present loss. It is human psychology. After 2015 Kerry gave many public speeches bemoaning the global community's failure to live up to the commitments made in Paris.[129]

COP21 did not produce a stable grand climate coalition. Psychological issues stood in the way of an agreement to create an effective carbon club.

After COP21 economists began to call more publicly for pricing carbon. In particular, Janet Yellen and Mark Carney, both of whom had headed central banks (Yellen in the United States and Carney in Canada and the UK) coauthored a G30 report emphasizing pricing carbon dioxide.[130]

In 2021, a few months before COP26, which took place in Glasgow, Scotland, Kerry stated in an interview that President Biden was considering supporting a carbon tax. At the time Kerry served as the US special presidential envoy for climate. The agenda for COP26 included tying up a loose end from the Paris agreement, so-called Article 6, which dealt with the price of carbon. Some progress was made at COP26 on Article 6; however, the agreement fell short of actually establishing a global price for carbon and did not come close to producing a stable grand coalition carbon club.

In Section 3 I discussed Buchanan's proposal to use clubs as a way to avoid the combination of uniform tax rates and lump sum wealth transfers when addressing free rider issues. Because Nordhaus' carbon club proposal uses a uniform carbon tax, it will be generally necessary to deal with wealth transfers. Within the UNFCCC framework such wealth transfers are described by the term "loss and damage." Prior to COP27 which took place in 2022, very little progress was made in COP meetings on any kind of loss and damage agreement. However, the parties at COP27 did manage to arrive at an agreement to provide "loss and damage" funding for vulnerable countries that are significantly impacted by climate disasters. Nevertheless, the outcome is a far cry from the achievement of a stable grand coalition carbon club.

Figure 22 compares several trajectories, with their associated confidence bands, provided by the website Our World in Data. At the top the case of

---

[129] In 2023 the *Wall Street Journal* editorial board opined about his remarks at the annual Davos conference. See Editorial Board, "John Kerry Lays It All Out on Climate Change: Biden's Envoy Calls for a World War II–Like Mobilization," January 19, 2023. https://bit.ly/3YHX65P.

[130] The report is available at https://tinyurl.com/3rsy6yya.

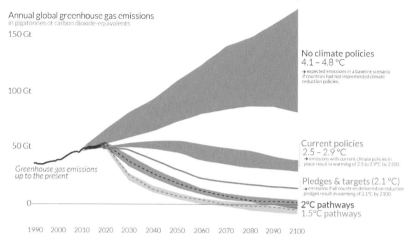

Figure 22 Comparison of trajectories for greenhouse gas emissions and associated temperature projections.

Source: Our World in Data. https://tinyurl.com/578792pa

behavioral business-as-usual lies within the group labeled "No climate policies." At the bottom are the trajectories required to maintain the global temperature below 1.5°C and 2°C respectively. Above those trajectory groups are "Pledges and targets" related to the Paris agreement. Those trajectories are associated with the temperature rising to 2.1°C.

The trajectory group "Current policies" fails to honor pledges and targets and is consistent with the metaphor of the Paris agreement being akin to a New Year's resolution. At the same time, "Current policies" constitutes an improvement of a sort over trajectories associated with business-as-usual behaviors. It remains to be seen what the future brings, given global events such as pandemics and military conflicts.[131]

Earlier in the section I mentioned a series of biased estimates by the IPCC. In addition to these, the IPCC underestimated growth of emissions from developing countries such as China and India, as well as the failure of developed countries such as the United States to institute effective abatement policies.

---

[131] As I discussed in Section 3, Nordhaus proposed the idea of a "carbon club" whereby large countries would require potential smaller trading partners to engage in low-emission behavior if they wish to trade with members of the club. In 2022 the EU instituted the Carbon Border Adjustment Mechanism (CBAM) in an attempt to place a fair price on the carbon emitted during the production of carbon intensive goods that enter the EU.

Given the discussion in this section and Section 2, there is good reason to be concerned about history repeating.

The ratio of net emissions to GDP is a measure of how "dirty" economic production is, whether for the world economy or the economy of a single country. For the period 2021 through 2025 the DICE-2016 estimate of the emissions intensity associated with behavioral business as usual is 0.31 kilograms of CO_2 per dollar. In 2021 the actual global emissions intensity of GDP was 0.35.[132] Nordhaus' underestimate is a continuation of the excessive optimism about the behavioral business-as-usual trajectory that is reflected in Figure 19.

Nordhaus has also been excessively optimistic about the global community being able to price carbon at its social cost. For the period 2021 through 2025 the optimal emission intensity from DICE-2016 is 0.25, which obviously is much lower than 0.35. Notably, the optimal intensity based on Stern's assumptions is even lower at 0.12. All of this implies that the current emission intensity of 0.35 is far too high by a factor between 40 percent and 190 percent.

China is a major reason the current emission intensity is so high. China has the second largest economy in the world behind the United States and China is the largest emitter of GHGs in the world. China's emissions continue to grow, in contrast to the United States and the EU, whose emissions have been on a downward trajectory. China has indicated that by 2030 its emissions will begin to decline and it will achieve net zero carbon emissions by 2060.

Notably, the US emission intensity is 0.2, which lies between the two aforementioned figures, 0.12 and 0.25. Estimates of China's emission intensity ratio vary but appear to be between 70 percent and 200 percent higher than that of the United States.[133] At the same time, China is also the global leader in investment and adoption of alternative energy, a point mentioned in Section 4. Certainly, alternatives have served to reduce China's net emissions, although the trend has remained positive.

The issue of present bias looms large for China. Present bias entails a reluctance to accept a reduction in near-term benefits associated with stronger abatement. In July 2023 President Xi Jinping rejected a suggestion from John Kerry for China to institute more aggressive abatement policies. Kerry's visit to China coincided with temperatures hitting a record high for a two-week period.

---

[132] Robert Litterman, "Catalyzing Private Financial Markets," conference presentation, Santa Clara University, June 9, 2023. "Catalyzing Private Financial Markets for Climate Solutions." Conference organized by University of California, Santa Cruz and Santa Clara University.

[133] Adjusting GDP to reflect purchasing power parity leads to a higher value for China's GDP. See Ana Swanson, "The Contentious U.S.-China Relationship, by the Numbers," *New York Times*, July 7, 2023. https://tinyurl.com/3bpnpuf2. In turn this lowers the estimate of the emissions intensity ratio.

Remarkably, China's response to rising heat has been to increase reliance on air conditioning, which is powered by electricity, which in turn has been fueled by burning more coal.[134] As I pointed out in the previous paragraph, China's economy is much "dirtier" than that of the United States and this is a big part of why the global economy has continued to follow a behavioral business-as-usual trajectory.

There is every reason to expect present bias to be strong, not only in developing countries but also in the United States and possibly Europe. In 2022 the US Supreme Court ruled stripped the EPA of its ability to regulate the fossil fuel industry. Republicans continue to resist policies aimed at emissions abatement and exercise that resistance when they have the political power to do it. As for Europe, which has a history of putting abatement policies into place, there are questions about how it will deal with growing political and economic instability, especially in connection with its reliance on natural gas from Russia.

I would note that pricing carbon dioxide need not be done explicitly. There are many types of taxes on fossil fuels, such as gasoline prices. There are also large subsidies from governments to fossil fuel producers.[135] Some economists have investigated the total net tax on fossil fuels, including all taxes and subsidies.[136] Such an analysis suggests that for 2019 the average price of carbon dioxide across the globe was about $19 per metric ton. This implicit price is considerably more than the $3 explicit price in the IMF analysis. Still, $19 is almost 50 percent less than Nordhaus' DICE-2016 recommended price, let alone his more recent $100 price, and of course the *Stern Review*'s much higher recommended price. I should add that global carbon subsidies are approximately $11 per metric ton. Removal of these subsidies would lead the global price of carbon to rise to about $30.

Psychology and politics, more than economists' recommendations based on IAMs, have driven climate policies. A vivid example involves the attempt by French president Emmanuel Macron to increase fuel taxes. The result was a very strong set of protests by grassroots populists wearing yellow vests to symbolize the working class. The protests were sufficiently disruptive to induce President Macron to withdraw the fuel tax.

The imposition of fuel taxes to mitigate anthropogenic global warming presents self-control challenges, which, as Irving Fisher pointed out, are

---

[134] See https://tinyurl.com/2p8p72eb.

[135] See Johannes Urpelainen and Elisha George, "Reforming Global Fossil Fuel Subsidies: How the United States Can Restart International Cooperation," Brookings Institution, July 14, 2021. https://bit.ly/45BJBH5.

[136] Mark Carhart, Bob Litterman, Clayton Munnings, and Olivia Vitali, "Measuring Comprehensive Carbon Prices of National Climate Policies," Working Paper, Kepos Capital, 2021.

especially strong for low-income households. There is every reason to believe that self-control and politics will continue to impact climate policy. This is not to say that economists' IAMs are immaterial. The IPCC continues to monitor the economics literature for insights.[137] However, thus far, the models have had at most a second-order impact on climate policy.

5.8 Key Takeaways

The big behavioral question in this section is why GHG emissions and carbon prices have followed behavioral business-as-usual trajectories instead of trajectories recommended by the IAMs developed by economists. The main takeaway from this long section is that the interplay between psychology and politics, not economic cost-benefit analysis, has been the key driver of real-world climate policy.

The psychological forces underlying humans' response to anthropogenic climate change are very strong, particularly procrastination that stems from self-control challenges such as present bias and trusting to luck. Behaving rationally does not come naturally to most people and therefore it is critical to understand the constraints on policy that arise because of human psychology.

Sensibly addressing the threat from global warming requires collective action by governments and appropriate regulation. Such action will need to address the free-rider problem. Indeed, Nordhaus' carbon club theory indicates that a collective solution is feasible for a carbon price trajectory that is in line with the optimal case from DICE-2016, though not for the trajectory prescribed by the *Stern Review*.

When Nordhaus articulated his carbon club theory in 2015, he was hopeful that a grand carbon coalition might arise from a Kyoto-like conference. In this regard, he wrote of "hopes that arrangements like the Kyoto Protocol will lead to deep emissions reductions." Nevertheless, no such collective solution has emerged. This is unsettling.

Notably, the free-rider issue also applies to the situation involving the "ozone hole." Somehow the global community came together to form a grand coalition around banning chlorofluorocarbons. However, there are important psychological differences between the situation involving ozone depletion and that of global warming.

---

[137] See Jim Skea, Priyadarshi Shukla, Alaa Al Khourdajie, and David McCollum, "Intergovernmental Panel on Climate Change: Transparency and Integrated Assessment Modeling," *WIREs Clim Change*, 2021. 12:e727. wires.wiley.com/climatechange. https://doi .org/10.1002/wcc.727. McCollum, at Oak Ridge National Laboratories, notes that the IPCC does not itself use IAMs. Instead the authors of the various IPCC chapters assess that literature and synthesize the relevant data, findings, and insights. Broadly speaking, there are two types of IAMs: (1) process-based (cost-effectiveness) IAMs; and (2) cost-benefit IAMs such as those discussed in this Element.

Psychological obstacles to addressing global warming surfaced right after the release of the Charney report. In the United States Ronald Reagan's perspective that "government is the problem" not only served as the key factor inhibiting climate action in the 1980s: It became enshrined in the ensuing decades as a libertarian principle and was reinforced by motivated reasoning to generate doubt, skepticism, and active resistance to the formulation and implementation of cost-benefit–based abatement policies. The end result was very strong present bias. This bias is ubiquitous and especially evident in China, whose emissions are the largest in the world and continue to grow.

To draw on Irving Fisher's leaky roof analogy, from the 1980s through the first two decades of the twentieth century, the global community did nothing substantial to fix the leaks in the roof when the weather was dry. Now that the 2020s have arrived, it has begun to drizzle and the leaks have gotten bigger. In a few spots pools of water have already formed. The global community is beginning work on the leaks, but barely so. Heavy rain is in the forecast, and there is a good chance that repairs will have to be made in the middle of storms. Unless the global community beats the odds, the outcome will be very messy. The big behavioral question is only getting bigger.

6 Hope for Reversing Global Warming

The big behavioral question notwithstanding, there is hope for a future in which humans reverse global warming and restore atmospheric GHG concentrations to their preindustrial levels. There is hope of being able to accomplish this feat by or before the end of the current century.

The hope will come from new technology, as the odds are low for the establishment of a global price for carbon that is in line with recommendations made by mainstream economists. For this reason the hope from new technology will be cautious hope, meaning hope tempered by fear.

Psychologically, hope is an emotion similar to optimism. However, people who are hopeful need not hold excessively optimistic beliefs, even if they act as if they do. By this I mean that hope is the expression of a preference as opposed to a judgmental error. Analogous statements apply to fear and pessimism.

Think back to the Ehrlich–Simon debate and Nordhaus' caution about not setting too high a carbon price early on. As I mentioned in Section 4, Nordhaus' warning pertained to the possible emergence of yet-to-be imagined technologies during the first half of the current century. New technologies for alternative energy sources and GHG removal are indeed emerging.

Financing the development of new GHG removal technologies might be critical. The global community has been making progress, albeit slow progress, on the financial front. For example, at COP26, the Glasgow Financial Alliance for Net Zero (GFANZ), a group of private financial institutions representing 40 percent of the world's financial assets, pledged to meet the goals set out in the Paris climate agreement.

The agreement reached at COP26 also tied up a loose end associated with Article 6, which was left unresolved in the Paris accords negotiated at COP21. Among other items, Article 6 provides the structure for a global offset market in GHG credits. Of course such a market puts a price on carbon. If done correctly, offsets provide agents with the option of "make or buy" when it comes to reducing emissions. They "make" when they reduce emissions directly. They "buy" when they purchase credits on the market for offsets from other agents who are "making" emission reductions.

Firms involved in GHG emissions, who do not remove GHGs as side activities from other profitable operations, and who lack sufficient government backing, might need to rely on the market for offsets in order to generate revenue. As I mentioned in Section 5, at COP27 there was progress on achieving an agreement about loss and damage payments from developed countries to the third world.

There are two parallel markets for offsets. One is called the compliance market, where agents operate in regulated environments with emissions caps. The other is the voluntary market, where agents are not required by regulation to reduce emissions but instead volunteer to purchase credits.

At present prices in the voluntary market are much lower than in the compliance market. This is consistent with the evidence about impact investing and ESG generally. Investors appear reluctant to sacrifice significant financial returns in exchange for ESG benefits.[138] Indeed, many ESG investors choose to concentrate their portfolios in ESG products because they believe such products will generate above-average financial returns.

All of this is to say that GHG removal technology might still require pricing carbon at prices that are considerably higher than the prices implied by the behavioral business-as-usual case. I say "might still require" because there is an important set of conditions whereby GHG concentrations decline without carbon prices needing to be high.

The conditions in question occur when costs are low for providing new energy alternatives and removing GHGs from the atmosphere. This is the hope, absent the pricing of carbon at the levels recommended by mainstream economists. Keep in mind what Nordhaus stated in 1997 about it not being

---

[138] For a discussion of the magnitude of the ESG premium investors are willing to pay, see Malcolm Baker, Mark L. Egan, and Suproteem K. Sarkar, "How Do Investors Value ESG?" NBER Working Paper 30708, 2022.

possible "to introduce these wondrous technologies unless we increase the cost of energy," by which he meant the price of carbon.

6.1 Greenhouse Gas Removal, Integrated Assessment Models, Risk, and Uncertainty

There are two drivers underlying GHG restoration scenarios, which I discuss at length in the appendix to this section. The first driver is technological advance, which leads the cost associated with alternative energy to decrease quickly. The second advance is new technology for removing GHGs from the atmosphere. The acronym for GHG removal technology is GGR. When speaking about atmospheric carbon dioxide removal, I shall use the acronym CDR for carbon dioxide removal.[139]

In the context of Nordhaus' framework hope for technological advances involves a lower abatement cost function than the one specified in DICE-2016. In this respect, the DICE-2016 assumption is the abatement cost function declines by 2 percent per year. In addition, Nordhaus assumes that net negative emissions will not materialize before the year 2160. Hope for removing GHGs from the atmosphere involves the possibility of negative emissions becoming available much earlier than 2160.[140] As I discussed in Section 3, the treatment of net negative emissions in DICE is crude, a flat 20 percent reduction rate. In this section I discuss assumptions which are less crude.

Keep in mind that atmospheric concentrations of carbon dioxide and other GHGs are much higher than they have been for the preceding 800,000 years. Just achieving net zero emissions will not restore concentrations and temperatures to preindustrial times: Net emissions need to be negative for this to occur.

Momentum for carbon dioxide removal is building noticeably. In 2022 the IPCC released the Working Group III portion of its Sixth Assessment report. In covering the release of the report, media outlets such as National Public Radio (NPR) reported on three key elements: carbon dioxide removal and sequestration, ramped up reliance on alternative energy sources, and behavioral changes by households, firms, and governments. Corresponding coverage by the *Washington Post* provided additional details, emphasizing land as a storage site for carbon as well as the following four additional elements: making buildings more efficient, transforming urban environments to become cleaner and greener, increasing the use of electric vehicles, and investing in making the world a fairer place.[141]

---

[139] There is an evolving use of the term "carbon removal" to mean the removal of both carbon dioxide and methane.

[140] Under Nordhaus' assumptions, net zero emissions are achieved in 2115, and under the *Stern Review* assumptions, net zero emissions are achieved in 2045.

[141] See https://bit.ly/3sot2jB.

Because CDR and GGR are risky activities, it is important to have analytical economic risk-based frameworks to assess them.[142] One such model, developed by Cai, Judd, and Lontzek (2019), extends Nordhaus' DICE framework to include uncertainty.[143] In doing so, the authors generalize the power utility function in DICE for the purpose of separating risk aversion and the elasticity of intertemporal consumption (EIS).[144]

Cai, Judd, and Lontzek make the argument that in the context of an optimal policy, the social cost of carbon will likely be high enough within the next decades to "remove carbon from the atmosphere." Notably, the trajectory for the social cost of carbon in their model is stochastic and significantly higher than the DICE counterpart. For 2005 their sensitivity analysis suggests a range for the social cost of carbon as $35–115 per ton. In contrast, Nordhaus' value based on DICE-2007 was $8.[145] For 2100 Cai, Judd, and Lontzek state that the expected social cost of carbon is $286, with there being a 10 percent probability of exceeding $700 and a 1 percent probability of exceeding $1,200. In contrast, the DICE-2016 counterpart is $271.

I should add that Cai, Judd, and Lontzek also modify the DICE damage function to feature tipping points. As I mentioned in Section 4, there is a literature addressing the uncertainty surrounding the damage function.[146] By "uncertainty," I mean "ambiguity," a lack of knowledge about the underlying

[142] The CDR and GGR activities, on a global scale, can pose significant risks that need to be analyzed carefully. See the comments of Wil Burns, Founding Co-executive Director of the Institute for Carbon Removal Law & Policy at American University in Washington, DC. https://tinyurl.com/bdhysw49.

[143] Yongyang Cai, Kenneth L. Judd, and Thomas S. Lontzek, "The Social Cost of Carbon with Economic and Climate Risks," *Journal of Political Economy* 127(6) (2019), 2684–2734. Insurance is a major issue for the handling of all kinds of risk, and climate risk is no exception. See www.youtube.com/watch?v=vjULeeoXaFI&t=2601s.

[144] Cai, Judd, and Lontzek (2019) generalize the power utility function in DICE to the Epstein–Zin recursive utility, for the purpose of separating risk aversion and the elasticity of intertemporal consumption (EIS). The axioms of expected utility theory pertain to rational behavior. See Larry G. Epstein and Stanley E. Zin, "Substitution, Risk Aversion, and the Temporal Behavior of Consumption and Asset Returns: A Theoretical Framework," *Econometrica* 57(4) (1989), 937–969. Epstein and Zin write that "this paper integrates a broad class of these non-expected utility theories" (p. 938).

[145] See https://tinyurl.com/46bxzhjb.

[146] In particular, uncertainty about the specification of the damage function will also lead to a higher trajectory for the social cost of carbon, relative to DICE-2016. See Ivan Rudik, "Optimal Climate Policy When Damages Are Unknown," *American Economic Journal: Economic Policy* 12(2) (2020), 340–373. https://doi.org/10.1257/pol.20160541. See also Robert S. Pindyck, "Uncertain Outcomes and Climate Change Policy," *Journal of Environmental Economics and Management* 63(3) (2012), 289–303; Robert S. Pindyck, "Climate Change Policy: What Do the Models Tell Us?" *Journal of Economic Literature* 51(3) (2013), 860–872; and Robert S. Pindyck, "The Use and Misuse of Models for Climate Policy." *Review of Environmental Economics and Policy* 11(1) (2017), 100–114.

functional form and parameter values associated with modeling climate damage.[147]

While these comparisons hearken back to the discussion of the Nordhaus–Stern debate in Section 4, the important point to remember is the following. The differences in estimates of the social cost of carbon are of little significance if psychological pitfalls lead the actual trajectories to be much closer to behavioral business-as-usual than to associated optima from any of these models. On account of this last point, we will need to place a great deal of hope in CDR and GGR.[148]

In respect to behavioral business-as-usual, keep in mind that while carbon dioxide emission rates have peaked in the United States and Europe, they have continued to grow elsewhere. China is the largest emitter and its emission rate continues to grow. New satellite technology provides clear evidence of locations within China that are associated with high emissions.[149] On the flip side, China is the largest investor in alternative energy, thereby providing some hope that before long China will emulate the United States and Europe in emission rates. Still, there will be a great need for CDR and GGR.

6.2 Behavioral Risk Modeling Issues

Both DICE and generalizations of DICE such as the model developed by Cai, Judd, and Lontzek (2019) are neoclassical in nature. As such, they assume that the associated objective functions reflect unbiased estimates of the underlying stochastic processes. In contrast, the behavioral approach allows for the possibility of biased estimates of the underlying stochastic process, and nonoptimal decisions by economic agents. These are two separate issues to be addressed separately.

---

[147] Amos Tversky and Daniel Kahneman, "Advances in Prospect Theory: Cumulative Representation of Uncertainty," *Journal of Risk and Uncertainty* 5 (1992), 297–323. There are various approaches to modeling choice under uncertainty. One way is to consider the range of outcomes associated with each decision, focus on the worst-case outcome associated with each decision, and then choose the decision associated with the best of the worst cases. This is the "maximin" approach. A less conservative approach is to use Choquet integrals and rank dependent utility. In this approach, for every decision, a subjective cumulative weighting is modified to over weight "capacities," the counterpart to cumulative probabilities, which are associated with the least favorable outcomes. As with maximin, rank dependent utility emphasizes the most unfavorable outcomes, but unlike maximin attaches some weight to more favorable outcomes than the worst.

[148] Cai, Judd, and Lontzek state the following: "Policy discussions today about R&D investment in developing those technologies should not compare the expected social cost of carbon in the future with the expected results of R&D investments, but should focus instead on the present value of having such technologies in those states of the world where the SCC justifies their deployment."

[149] Raymond Zhong, "Who's Driving Climate Change? New Data Catalogs 72,000 Polluters and Counting," *New York Times*, November 9, 2022, updated November 15, 2022. https://tinyurl.com/5n7etdyk.

6.2.1 Biased Estimates, Sentiment

To accommodate biased estimates of the underlying stochastic process, an additional term is added to the log-stochastic discount rate function. This term is a log-change of measure, which captures the impact of behavioral errors such as excessive optimism and overconfidence. The log-change of measure reflects sentiment.

Neoclassical stochastic discount functions are typically downward-sloping functions of the consumption growth rate. However, the addition of a log-change of measure to a neoclassical stochastic discount function can cause the resulting sum to oscillate or slope upward. The addition of sentiment to a neoclassical stochastic discount function typically increases the return variance associated with consumption growth. In consequence, sentiment tends to increase the consumption growth risk premium.

Nordhaus was clear to say that climate policy is constrained by the real-world behavior of agents. This is why he insists that the return on capital from DICE be in line with historical values. The same statement applies to the influence of sentiment, meaning judgmental errors.

6.2.2 Non-maximizing Firms

The neoclassical framework assumes that firms are profit maximizing. In contrast, the behavioral approach recognizes that psychological pitfalls, such as excessive optimism and overconfidence, often prevent firms' managers from choosing value-maximizing strategies. In this regard, the phenomenon "sensitivity of investment to cash flow" entails firms increasing investment when they are flush with cash and reducing investment when not. Although this pattern can stem from market frictions, it is also correlated with managerial biases such as excessive optimism and overconfidence.

Non-maximizing behavior is especially important for firms engaged in CDR and GGR. Consider an example involving solar energy.[150] Solar energy firm Solyndra manufactured cylindrical solar panels that while expensive to produce were easy to install on the roofs of commercial buildings.

Solyndra was founded in 2004. By March 2009 Solyndra had raised approximately $650 million in private equity financing as well as $535 million in debt that was guaranteed by the US government as part of a program to encourage clean energy. At the time, Solyndra had a single manufacturing facility but was planning to build a second. Later that year Solyndra filed an IPO registration

---

[150] The discussion about Solyndra is taken from Hersh Shefrin, *Behavioral Corporate Finance*, second edition (New York: McGraw-Hill Education, 2018).

statement, which it withdrew after investment bankers expressed concern about declining prices for electricity.

Nevertheless, the firm built a second, larger facility. The *Washington Post* quoted a former engineer at the firm as saying that after receiving the loan guarantee, Solyndra spent money "left and right" and that the cash infusion "made people sloppy." Notably, the firm built its second facility despite growth in unsold inventory at its first facility. Moreover, Solyndra's profit margin at the time was negative and worsening. In 2011 the firm filed for Chapter 11 bankruptcy. Given the active role the US government will play in future financing of alternative energy, it is worthwhile remembering the lessons about excessive optimism and overconfidence from the Solyndra case.[151]

Solar firms like Solyndra, if their technologies were successful, held the potential to compete successfully in the market for electric power. By successfully compete, I mean that they were capable of generating revenues and profits by selling power to customers. The situation with CDR and GGR firms is more complex because they need to find agents willing to pay them to remove GHGs from the atmosphere and sequester these gases where appropriate. There are a host of technical and social obstacles to address as well.[152]

6.3 Key Takeaways

Embedded within DICE-2016 are assumptions about technological progress in respect to both alternative energy and GHG removal. These assumptions impact the model's estimated emissions trajectories associated with two cases, the first being when carbon is priced at the social cost of carbon and the second being when carbon is priced in accordance with business-as-usual behavior.

The big behavioral question is to explain the gap between the two cases, with this question becoming bigger, meaning that the estimated gap is wider than previously thought. This means that the global community will have to hope that actual technological progress on alternative energy and GHG removal will be greater than what the DICE-assumptions stipulate.

---

[151] The Solyndra issue pertains both to firm behavior and to public policy. For an example featuring wind power, see Pejman Bahramian, Glenn P. Jenkins, and Frank Milne, "The Displacement Impacts of Wind Power Electricity Generation: Costly Lessons from Ontario," *Energy Policy* 152(112211) (2021), 1–8. The issue here involves more expensive wind power displacing less expensive hydroelectric power. For an example of transition risk from decarbonization in the state of Washington, see James Conca, "Washington State's Approaching Energy Crisis: Good Intentions Gone Wrong," *Forbes*, June 15, 2021. https://tinyurl.com/2d8tj55t.

[152] See June Sekera and Andreas Lichtenberger, "Assessing Carbon Capture: Public Policy, Science, and Societal Need: A Review of the Literature on Industrial Carbon Removal," *Biophysical Economics and Sustainability* (2020), 5–14. https://doi.org/10.1007/s41247-020-00080-5.

New, improved IAMs explicitly incorporate risk. This is an important advance, as new technologies are inherently risky, as are climate damages and other economic outcomes. The new IAMs generate much higher values for the social cost of carbon than DICE, plausibly by a factor of four. Moreover, there is evidence that carbon continues to be priced in the range of 6 percent to 10 percent of its social cost, a range consistent with DICE assumptions.

Psychological biases, especially present bias, lie at the root of my analysis of the big behavioral question. In particular, these biases explain the reluctance to use taxes to price GHGs in line with their respective social costs. This reluctance is an unsettling behavior, and results in abatement being more costly than necessary, plausibly by a factor of five to seven.[153] The cost of reluctance is a behavioral cost, and it is large.

The Charney report from 1979 alerted the global community that it was in the domain of losses. As a result, present bias was compounded by trusting to luck, the aversion to accepting a sure loss, which increases the propensity to accept bets which are imprudent. Thus far, the associated bets have not paid off. The global community's willingness to accept imprudent risks has only grown.

There is much to be concerned about, given the heavy reliance we are placing on technology. My hope is that I will be surprised that it all ends well. Hope based on technology is fine, but there is a risk that it will be insufficient and this is unsettling. The global community needs to face up to the big behavioral question and to the magnitude of the costs associated with psychological biases that obstruct the implementation of good climate policies. If not, the consequences will be very unsettling.

---

[153] This point is discussed in the appendix to Section 4.

Acknowledgments

I dedicate this Element to my wife and inspiration, Arna. She has been my life partner from the time I was an undergraduate developing a keen interest in environmental issues.

I very much thank Riccardo Rebonato, the editor of the Elements series, whose excellent comments led me to shape the Element in the way that I did. I thank Chris Harrison, my editor at Cambridge University Press, whose editorial expertise and knowledge of climate change has helped me improve the exposition.

I have benefited from conversations about global warming with many people. In particular, I thank Peter Fiekowsky for his vision of climate restoration and for sharing with me details of the models he employs to study GHG removal. I also wish to acknowledge discussions with Donald Addu, Spencer Anderson, David Bostwick, Enrico Cervellati, Brent Constantz, Erica Dodds, Dougal Heap, David Gautschi, Kesten Green, Steve Keen, Kristin Kusanovich, Anthony Leiserowitz, Derek Lemoine, Bob Litterman, Ed Maibach, Emilie Mazzacurati, David McCollum, Frank Milne, Dana Nucciltelli, Billy Pizer, Helen Popper, Terri Pugh, Josh Santos, Gavin Schmidt, June Sekera, William Sundstrom, and Rick Wayman.

I thank Santa Clara University for its support in making this publication available as Open Access on Cambridge Core.

Cambridge Elements $\equiv$

Quantitative Finance

Riccardo Rebonato
EDHEC Business School

Editor Riccardo Rebonato is Professor of Finance at EDHEC Business School and holds the PIMCO Research Chair for the EDHEC Risk Institute. He has previously held academic positions at Imperial College, London, and Oxford University and has been Global Head of Fixed Income and FX Analytics at PIMCO, and Head of Research, Risk Management and Derivatives Trading at several major international banks. He has previously been on the Board of Directors for ISDA and GARP, and he is currently on the Board of the Nine Dot Prize. He is the author of several books and articles in finance and risk management, including *Bond Pricing and Yield Curve Modelling* (2017, Cambridge University Press).

About the Series

Cambridge *Elements in Quantitative Finance* aims for broad coverage of all major topics within the field. Written at a level appropriate for advanced undergraduate or graduate students and practitioners, *Elements* combines reports on original research covering an author's personal area of expertise, tutorials and masterclasses on emerging methodologies, and reviews of the most important literature.

Cambridge Elements ≡

Quantitative Finance

Printed in the United States
by Baker & Taylor Publisher Services